Live Colorfully

Barbara Bargeati

A
Colorful
Way of
Living

How to Be More,

Create More,

Do More the

Vera Bradley Way

BARBARA BRADLEY BAEKGAARD

Cofounder, designer, and chief creative officer of Vera Bradley

A Colorful Way of Living

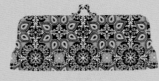

ST. MARTIN'S PRESS NEW YORK

A COLORFUL WAY OF LIVING. Copyright © 2017 by Barbara Bradley Baekgaard. All rights reserved. Printed in the United States of America. For information, address St. Martin's Press, 175 Fifth Avenue, New York, N.Y. 10010.

www.stmartins.com

Designed by Laura Klynstra

The Library of Congress Cataloging-in-Publication Data is available upon request.

ISBN 978-1-250-12191-2 (hardcover)
ISBN 978-1-250-12192-9 (e-book)

Our books may be purchased in bulk for promotional, educational, or business use. Please contact your local bookseller or the Macmillan Corporate and Premium Sales Department at 1-800-221-7945, extension 5442, or by e-mail at MacmillanSpecialMarkets@macmillan.com.

First Edition: April 2017

10 9 8 7 6 5 4 3 2 1

For my mother, Vera,

my children and grandchildren,

and for the sisterhood of women

who honor my mother's name

by carrying Vera Bradley bags and designs.

This book is for you.

CONTENTS

INTRODUCTION: It's Never Too Late ⤳ **XI**

COLOR YOUR PERSPECTIVE

Ready, Fire, Aim ⤳ **3**

Sell Yourself First ⤳ **9**

Know Your Strengths ⤳ **15**

The Best Idea Wins ⤳ **21**

Define Success ⤳ **25**

Keep the *F* in Fun ⤳ **29**

Slip Up from Time to Time ⤳ **37**

It's Good to Be a Girl ⤳ **41**

Know Your Audience ⤳ **45**

COLOR YOUR RELATIONSHIPS

Choose Nice ∿ **53**

Titles Mean (Almost) Nothing ∿ **57**

Invite Connection ∿ **61**

Be a Friend, Make a Friend ∿ **67**

Practice Kindness ∿ **73**

Open Doors ∿ **79**

Keep It Real ∿ **83**

Choose Carefully ∿ **87**

COLOR YOUR WORK

Find Your Inspiration ∿ **95**

Go Big ∿ **101**

There's Enough for Everyone ∿ **107**

Act as If ∾ **111**

Sometimes Wrong, Never in Doubt ∾ **115**

Cultivate a Sisterhood ∾ **121**

The Culture of Color ∾ **125**

Add a Big Cause to Your Purpose ∾ **129**

Give Just for Fun ∾ **137**

COLOR YOUR EVERY DAY

Be Fussy ∾ **145**

Refine Your Tastes ∾ **151**

Define Your Style ∾ **155**

Keep Moving & Allow for Little Extras ∾ **161**

Make Yum Yum Cake ∾ **167**

Cultivate New Friendships ∾ **173**

COLOR YOUR LIFE

Find Your Balance ⤳ **179**

Follow Love ⤳ **185**

Remember Romance ⤳ **191**

Celebrate Your Place in the World ⤳ **193**

Discontinue Old Patterns ⤳ **197**

Cut and Trim ⤳ **203**

Continue to Redesign ⤳ **207**

Embrace Your Success ⤳ **211**

Find the Silver Lining ⤳ **215**

Lean on Your Sisters ⤳ **221**

Notice the Magical Moments ⤳ **229**

Acknowledgments ⤳ **233**

Author Bio ⤳ **237**

Company Bio ⤳ **238**

INTRODUCTION

IT'S NEVER TOO LATE

In 1982, my good friend and neighbor Pat Miller and I were sitting in the Atlanta airport, sharing a bag of M&M'S and flipping through fashion magazines on a long layover from Miami. We were returning from a girl-friends' getaway to celebrate my dad's eighty-second birthday and play outdoor tennis at a time of year when most people were wrapped up in winter scarves. Now into our third hour of waiting at the gate for our connecting flight home, something struck us: we were looking at a procession of *boring*. Of the hundreds of travelers parading by, everyone—both men and women—had the same characterless black bags. Some were big and some were small. Some were rolled and some were carried. But they were all, every last one of them, boring.

I turned to Pat and said, "This airport could sure use a splash of color, don't you think? I haven't seen a single piece of luggage that's cheerful or . . ."

"Fun," Pat finished my sentence.

This wasn't a new conversation for us. Before leaving for our trip we'd both complained that we had nothing suitable in which to pack our weekend clothes. Our luggage was big and bulky, colorless, nearly shapeless, and without one feminine detail. What we'd wished for was a simple and attractive getaway bag with several compartments for cosmetics, jewelry, and shoes—preferably in a bright color that matched where we were going.

"What if," I asked, "we made colorful overnight bags *for women just like us?*"

Pat jumped at the idea.

We'd gone into business together before. When I'd moved to Fort Wayne almost twenty years previously, Pat was the first to show up at my doorstep and welcome me to the neighborhood. Never mind that I was holding a wallpaper brush when I invited her in. "The first thing I do when I move into a new house is wallpaper," I explained. "It's the quickest way I know of to add color and charm. It makes a house feel like a home." When Pat said she'd always wanted to learn how to hang paper, I handed her a brush, and that's how I made my first friend in my new hometown.

Not long after that, Pat joined me in hanging wallpaper in homes throughout Fort Wayne. We did this during the day while our children were in school to bring in a little extra pocket money. I'd had a similar side business with another friend when I lived in Chicago. We called it Paper Dolls, and had dressed for the part in pink overalls and pink lipstick. We even waved pink paintbrushes like princess wands. It was a cute gimmick, but once I hit forty I figured I'd aged out of calling myself "doll." Pat and I brainstormed for a new name for our business and laughed to ourselves when we thought we'd landed on something perfect: Well Hung. Our husbands didn't appreciate the humor quite as much as we did, so we went back to the drawing board and finally settled on Up Your Wall.

Back at the airport, as Pat and I continued to observe the parade of travelers at our departure gate, we grew more and more excited by our new business idea. Women, we agreed, needed an alternative to the drab and uninspiring options in the luggage department. While we were both familiar with the popular brands Laura Ashley and Pierre Deux (one British and the other French), their travel totes were not available in Indiana, or anywhere else in the Midwest. That's when we knew we were onto something.

My mother, Vera Bradley,

inspired us all with her style and elegance.

As our idea to create a new line of American bags and accessories began to take shape, we realized this was an opportunity to take our lives in a colorful new direction at the time. I was a forty-three-year-old stay-at-home mom. I'd had four children in my first five years of marriage *(whew!* is right), and while I'd dabbled in different things over the years, I'd never had a career. I was ready for more.

Where other women may have identified the same market and talked themselves out of the opportunity, Pat and I decided to go for it. To start before we stopped. On our plane ride back to Fort Wayne we eagerly chatted about patterns, fabrics, and colors. In the following week—much to the horror of anyone who has ever gone to business school—we started our company without a budget or a business plan, and only five hundred dollars between us that we'd borrowed from our husbands. (Believe it or not, I'm from a generation where your husband gave you an allowance, even for groceries.) Before anyone could talk us out of it—including each another—we drove to Jo-Ann's Fabrics with cash in hand and bought as many yards of cotton material as we could afford. We took the fabric back to my basement and began cutting out Simplicity patterns on my family's Ping-Pong table. We started with three simple pieces: a barrel-shaped handbag, a duffel, and a garment bag. All three pieces were functional, feminine, *and* colorful. Exactly what we'd wished for when we'd packed for our trip to Miami.

We named the company Vera Bradley after my mother, a former Elizabeth Arden model, a woman who stood out from the crowd for her classic style, and who radiated an unwavering enthusiasm for living a bright and colorful life. Pat and I agreed that Vera embodied the values and style of the company we wanted to create.

Within the first year of starting our business, Pat and I sold ten thousand dollars' worth of product. That number rose to a million by the third year. Today—some thirty-five years later—Vera Bradley has over half a billion dollars of annual revenue. Not bad for an idea that came to life at a departure gate.

Where financial success is always a perk, this wasn't our motivation for starting Vera Bradley. We simply had a fun idea to create a product that brought us enjoyment, and, as an added bonus, would make other women happy, too. And also we were ready for more—to be more, create more, and do more—to live a bigger and more colorful life. How about you? Are *you* ready for more color?

M y name is Barbara Bradley Baekgaard and I'm a wife, mother, sister, friend, and grandmother. I'm also the cofounder and chief creative officer of Vera Bradley. Perhaps you're someone who's been carrying our totes and backpacks since college. Or maybe you first noticed our weekender bags carried by women throughout airports and train stations all over the country. If, on the other hand, you're not yet familiar with me or my company, then I'm happy to finally meet you.

In the three-plus decades since forming Vera Bradley, I've met and spoken with countless women like you and I'm frequently asked about that pivotal moment in the Atlanta airport—was I nervous or scared to attempt to create a business from virtually nothing, especially in midlife? The truth is that I felt quite the opposite. I was thrilled by the possibility of creating something more for myself and making the time to give it my all. Of course, in considering a change, my partner and I weren't looking to scrap all that we'd done before. We drew on our existing strengths, talent, and experience—an eye for color and design, a sense of what everyday women want, and good people skills—to make our new handbag company better than our last endeavor, and to make our personal redesign bigger and more satisfying than we ever could have imagined.

Imagine what *you* can do.

Whether you're a forty-something-year-old looking to change careers, a stay-at-home mom ready to get out of the house, a freshman in college, or an overworked twentysomething who worries you've already invested too much time and college money to go in a different direction, my message to you is this: no matter your age or where you are in your life, you can refine, redesign, and sometimes entirely reinvent yourself. You, too, can do more of what you love. And you don't necessarily have to give up a thing. You can build from where you are.

Whatever it is you're inspired to do—whether it's create art, dive deeper into an existing project or passion, pursue a new relationship, or move to a different city—you can redesign the details of your life and work at any age. All you need is to believe in your own potential to build on what you've already learned, pull out the courage to try something new, and stop second-guessing yourself. That's exactly what Pat and I did. We threaded the needle and went to work.

Was it really that simple?

It really was, which is why when I was first urged to write this book by my son-in-law Bob Hall (Bob's the chairman of the board for Vera Bradley), I looked at him skeptically. I've never thought that my way of doing things is all that different or that our company is really that unique. Nor do I claim to have all the answers. In writing a book, the last thing I wanted was to come off as some CCO pushing her legacy lessons, or worse—asserting her business manifesto.

"Isn't this all very obvious?" I asked Bob. "Isn't this how most companies get started?"

Bob laughed and said, "Barb, how would you know? You've never worked for any other company."

He had a point.

"And," he added, "in the world of business, you are one of the few women as successful as you are who didn't inherit her company or take venture capital to grow it. You and Pat created it from nothing. Without ever studying business, you turned five hundred bucks into half a billion. Your readers will want to know how you did this."

Assuming you do, I'll tell you. The same way you can similarly redesign the business and life of *your* dreams.

To get to the next step in your life, start by building on your strengths and values. Do you know what those are? The values that were imparted to me growing up in the house of Ed and Vera Bradley were the initial stitches, so to speak, that I wove into the larger design of my life. They are the very threads I've pulled from to design (and then redesign!) the pattern of my day-to-day world, and the company, too. They include:

- Cultivate chutzpah and take chances
- Make friends wherever you go
- Choose nice
- Notice the details
- Keep the *f* in fun
- Add a big cause to your purpose
- Lean on your sisters
- Slip up from time to time
- And remember always—there's enough success and happiness for everyone

When Pat and I started Vera Bradley, we hadn't studied market trends (not outside of the Atlanta airport, that is). We didn't have a designated demographic, nor had we even identified our "brand story." We simply built a sisterhood with bonds as strong as family, on our strengths and values. And every step of the way we continued to believe in what we were building and why we were doing it—to help make women's lives easier, and to also delight them at the same time. I know that's not what they teach in business school, but that's what we did.

Since I've always been better at telling stories than giving business and life advice, that's what I'll do in the pages ahead. I'll share with you what's worked for us, and while I recognize that our value-based style and practical approach might not speak to everyone, it has guided the direction of my life and the company for thirty-five years and continues to help me thrive in business, health, and relationships—every single day.

So, sit back and get comfy (in a beach chair, on a plane, tucked into bed, or in your best friend's guest room). I hope that what you read brings you inspiration, insight, and laughter—and perhaps the clarity and courage you need to make a change and live the beautiful and colorful life you dream of.

It's my honor to spend this time with you.

Color
Your
Perspective

READY, FIRE, AIM

When I speak about how Vera Bradley got started I say that my approach was "ready, fire, aim." At which point I'm often corrected by someone in the crowd who asks, "Don't you mean, 'ready, *aim,* fire'?"

"No," I reply with a smile. "I am where I am today because I'm not afraid to fire without a clear target in mind."

I'm a "shoot first, ask questions later" type of woman. That is, if I have an idea or a goal, if there's something that I've been inspired to do, I don't think or sit on it too long—I fire. That's certainly how Vera Bradley was born. My partner and I became excited by an idea one day and before anyone could talk us out of it we took action. If we'd sat around second-guessing ourselves and talking through every aspect of launching the company, there'd likely not be a Vera Bradley.

I consider this one of my strengths. But I realize that not everyone is like this. Take my brother Eddie. A professional musician, Eddie likes to joke that of all of us six

WE ARE ALL GRACED WITH MORE THAN ONE GOOD IDEA.

3

siblings, he's the one with the real talent in the family. Without a doubt Eddie possesses artistic gifts I just don't have. And to these gifts he adds a capacity for practice and planning. Eddie will spend hours in rehearsal, and always chooses the right music and the right venue for a performance. I prefer to wing it. Which may be why I can't play an instrument to save my life.

"But, Barbie," Eddie will encourage, "what *you've* got is all the chutzpah."

Fearless chutzpah like I'm describing can be a terrific asset and I exercise mine every chance I get, in every aspect of my career and personal life. That said, I know that not every idea will materialize, that not every dream comes true. That's okay. In fact, you should expect the occasional snag. And when you do, find comfort in the fact that another idea will come along, as it surely will. We are all graced with more than one good idea in our lives.

Before settling in Fort Wayne, my husband and I had moved every two years with his company. That's when I discovered that the quickest and the most inexpensive way to make a house feel like a home was to hang new wallpaper. If, after a few months, I decided I didn't like the pattern or color I'd selected, I'd take it down and try something new. I'm always willing to take a chance and even make a mistake, but I'm not willing to live with bare and colorless walls.

My point is that if your project falls flat or doesn't find completion, if your hard work doesn't pan out, or if you aren't recognized for your efforts—start again. Locate your own fearlessness, that "ready, fire, aim" attitude within *you*. Now, if fearlessness isn't something you always remember to throw into your bag, you may have to dig deep. It's easy to talk yourself out of something, with "I can't" or "I shouldn't" or "if only." But consider whose voice that is—is it really *yours*? Or is it the voice of someone around you? Naysayers can be discouraging, to say the least, which is why I always listen to myself first. My inner voice. My gut. And when it gives me an idea that I believe in and quietly nudges or strongly encourages me to fire, I listen. And then, nine times out of ten, I take a chance.

When my children were little and learning to ski, I used to tell them: if you're not falling, you're not trying hard enough. Try hard enough to fail. Commit to your new pursuit wholeheartedly and put all your fears and apprehensions about how, when, and where it's going to get done on the back shelf for now. In the very early days of Vera Bradley I used to say, "We don't have a problem until we have an order." Let's just get the business first and then figure out how to deliver.

There are many critics of my way of thinking, including everyone who has ever taken a business course. They say that my "ready, fire, aim" approach is too impulsive. Irresponsible, even. "You need a marketing strategy," they say. "You need future projections in test markets and some kind of plan before you begin any successful endeavor in business or in life."

But I'm living proof that that's not always the case. I don't mean to imply that analysis, research, and careful planning aren't necessary. I work with planners every day. In fact, I rely on them to help make Vera Bradley the company that it is and will be. But there comes a time when moving forward means actually moving, and I'll challenge any Fortune 500 CEO on this point.

My niece Kathy, who is a sales rep for Vera Bradley, has witnessed professionally and personally how my "ready, fire, aim" approach can play out. When she and her husband, Bryan, were looking to buy a new home in Fort Wayne she called me from the road in Michigan one day and asked me if I'd go look at a house that just came on the market. Real estate in the Fort Wayne area tends to sell quickly, so I understood why she didn't want to miss out on the opportunity to see it. I made an appointment to tour the house with the Realtor, and texted Kathy a few hours later with the following message: *Bought the house.*

> THERE COMES A TIME WHEN MOVING FORWARD MEANS ACTUALLY MOVING.

Not a minute later my phone rang. It was Kathy. "Aunt Barbie, I told you to go by the house, not *buy* the house!"

I explained that by the time I'd arrived at the open house, there were already several people interested. And because it seemed to be exactly what Kathy was envisioning and wanting for her family, I acted.

"If you don't like it," I said, "I'll help you flip it."

This might sound impulsive (Kathy initially thought so, until she agreed that the house was perfect for her family), but I believe that we miss too many opportunities when we hold ourselves back, debating and doubting and hedging our bets. I don't know about you, but there's only so much of this running around in mental circles I can do before I become dizzy. I'm very quick to arrive at a decision and anyone who works with me will attest to this, especially those who sit next to me in meetings. As the head of a public company I'm invited to my fair share, but sitting in a two-hour meeting is practically torture for me. I can sit still for about as long as it takes me to finish a cup of coffee. Then I get antsy. I must get up and walk around. A few paces around the table and I'm apt to interject. "These are all great ideas, but what I want to know is: what is the one thing we can do *today* that will make a difference and keep us moving forward?"

ASK YOURSELF:
what can you do today?

If fear and doubt weren't stopping you, how would your life look different from the one you are living right now? I encourage you to hang some wallpaper and see how it looks. If you don't like it, take it down and try something else. Be willing to take chances and even make mistakes in an effort to live more colorfully.

Sell Yourself First

Pat and I began selling Vera Bradley product right out of our homes to women in our neighborhood. Within several months, our initial small orders of ten to twenty duffels and handbags were doubling and tripling. From there, we solicited local specialty and gift shops. Nobson's in Fort Wayne was the first to carry Vera Bradley, and the orders came in faster than we could deliver them.

That's when Pat and I recognized that we needed more hands. So we placed an ad in the local paper for home sewers. The idea was that Pat and I would cut out all the fabric in my basement and the sewers would take the patterns home to complete. We hired a husband-and-wife team named Mark and Cindy (whom we referred to affectionately as "Mork and Mindy"). Bringing them on board helped immensely. Still, while they could quickly sew whatever we threw at them, we were running low on fabric and trim.

One afternoon, on what had become a routine trip to Jo-Ann Fabric, Pat and I found our solution. Stamped on the end of the roll of one of our more popular prints was the name of the wholesale distributor—VIP Fabrics, New York City.

Pat and me

in the early days of the company. We knew that we weren't
just selling a product, we were selling ourselves.

Of course! This is how we'd be able to afford the fabric we needed to fulfill our mounting orders. Pat and I agreed, "We need to buy directly from them."

The five hundred dollars that we'd borrowed from our husbands had all been spent. But while our initial start-up money was gone, we'd since received a generous gift from Marshall Miller, a friend of my husband's. We'd had dinner one night with Marshall and his wife during which I'd told them all about Pat's and my new company. Toward the end of the evening, Marshall took me aside and handed me a check for twenty-five hundred dollars. "If your company is a success," he said, "then this is a loan. If your company is a failure, then it's a gift. But I believe you're onto something and I believe in you." (I'm proud to say that we later paid him back the twenty-five hundred dollars.)

The next week, following our aha moment in JoAnn Fabric, I visited my daughter Amy at Marymount College in Tarrytown, New York. I figured; while I'm here why not drive into Manhattan to the downtown offices of VIP Fabrics? It hadn't even occurred to me to make an appointment. When the receptionist asked what company I was representing, I told her simply, "Vera Bradley." Not ten minutes later, Leo Driscoll, the vice president of sales, welcomed me into his office with a firm handshake and a smile. We made small talk for several minutes until the conversation turned toward business.

"So what can I do for you?" he asked.

I explained that I was interested in buying a hundred yards of one of their more popular prints. Leo looked at me with some confusion. He said, "You know that our minimum order is two thousand yards. Who did you say you were with again?"

"Vera Bradley," I replied cheerfully. "We're a small company based in Fort Wayne, Indiana. My friend Pat and I started it, and we're getting great response."

Leo looked even more befuddled. "I thought you were from Vera?"

"Oh." I smiled, quickly piecing together that the receptionist had mistaken me for someone from the much larger company known for their beautiful scarves and table linens, and whom Leo was probably hoping to add to his list of top accounts.

THE BEST WAY TO BUILD BUSINESS AND RELATIONSHIPS IS BY MAKING *YOURSELF* THE PRODUCT THAT YOU'RE SELLING.

"If you're not from Vera," he continued, "how the hell did you get in here?"

Through that door, is what I thought. But I shrugged and smiled. "I just did."

In that instant, Leo could have easily asked me to leave, but instead he sat back in his chair, and his expression shifted toward amusement. He started to laugh.

"You just did," he repeated back to me with a smile.

I'd used my people skills (and okay, a certain sense of well-timed naïveté) to get a seat in front of the vice president of sales, and now that I was here I decided to *just be me.*

My father, Ed Bradley, was a professional salesman his whole life. He loved everybody and everybody loved him. I believe that Dad was such a success because he knew that the best salespeople were the ones who didn't appear to be selling you anything. Now I happen to think that being a salesperson is a great thing. (I also think we're all salespeople to some extent.) Still, I know that for many people the stereotype of the pushy salesperson, the one who doesn't listen and who goes in for the hard sell, is the one that persists. Dad wasn't like that. He was approachable and real, always a gentleman. And his focus was on building relationships before sales. Dad knew that the best way to build business and relationships is by making *yourself* the product that you're selling. Of course, it was Dad who told me that "In business, you sell yourself first, your company second, and the product third." In other words—you can't sell anything until you sell *yourself.*

I took Dad's advice. I didn't try to "sell" Leo on anything or represent myself in any kind of false way (now that we'd cleared up which "Vera" I actually worked for). I believe Leo must have felt my authenticity because his overall business demeanor started to loosen up. He invited me to tell him more about our company and products, and by the end of our time together we were carrying on like old friends. Leo said he'd be willing to help us out and even though a hundred yards was inconsistent with their minimum order, he agreed to sell us some sample yardage at a negotiated rate. I stood up to leave and shook his hand. I'd successfully sold Leo on taking a chance on Vera Bradley, but really on taking a chance on me.

Dad would have loved *Shark Tank*, the reality TV show where a panel of venture-capital investors considers offers from aspiring entrepreneurs. In nearly every episode, if the "sharks" believe in the person and recognize their drive, they are more apt to invest in their company. This is exactly what happened to me. The day I walked into VIP unannounced marked the beginning of a long and very successful partnership with the company (in fact, Vera Bradley became VIP's largest client), as well as a lasting friendship with Leo, because I sold myself by *just being myself* from day one.

SELL *yourself* FIRST

Think about it—if people don't trust you or feel like they don't really know you, they won't want to do business with you, help you, or even share a meal with you. On the other hand, most people won't leave a job, a relationship or the dinner table if the personal connections feel real and good. In my experience, when you create personal relationships, you create opportunities that you didn't see coming.

In what areas of your life can you create stronger and more authentic connections by selling yourself first?

KNOW YOUR STRENGTHS

You can only truly sell yourself when you *know yourself*. In particular, when you know and follow your natural strengths and talents. So how to identify those strengths? Because I'm a business-book junkie (which is more a predilection than a talent), I turned to one of my favorites, the bestseller *StrengthsFinder 2.0*, and found that my top strengths are:

- positivity (I am upbeat and enthusiastic)
- adaptability (I live in the moment)
- developer (I see potential and growth)
- belief (I'm driven by my values)
- empathy (I can put myself in other people's shoes)

The premise of this popular evaluation is a rewrite of the you-can-be-anything-you-want-to-be maxim. The *StrengthsFinder 2.0* assessment argues that you *cannot* be anything you want to be—but you *can* be a lot more of who you already are. The test helps us discover and describe our unique talents so we can focus on what we do best. In my experience, knowing what my strengths are has allowed me to live and lead by my strong suit, and as a result, enjoy a greater sense of success and ease. I believe that if your work feels easy, it means you're operating from your strengths. Add to that my willingness to let others excel where I am not as strong has also helped me to achieve even more. Knowing your strengths includes recognizing—and admitting—where you're challenged.

You don't have to do *StrengthsFinder 2.0* to find out what you're good at. Start by asking yourself, "What do I enjoy doing?" "What seems to come naturally to me?" Sometimes an outside perspective helps; ask your friends and colleagues—people you trust and respect—to point out your strengths. Where all my life people have commented on my natural eye for design, I hesitate to call it a "strength" because for me, it's as effortless as combing my hair. Think about what comes that easy for you, or what is so enjoyable that you resist qualifying it as a talent. I see so many people who tirelessly, and with much frustration, try to be strong where they are not. What if you gave yourself permission to admit that you can't do *everything* well? And built only on what comes easy and naturally?

The first time I heard the term "Founder's syndrome" was an aha moment for me. Founder's syndrome occurs when an organization or team operates primarily according to the personality of the founders, which over time can become a limiting force rather than the creative and productive factor it was in the early days of the company. Well, that wasn't going to happen to Vera Bradley.

When the company was young, I shared with Pat my shortcomings in math and finance. While I felt confident that we could make beautiful products that would sell, I accepted that I didn't know the first thing about how to price the merchandise or even create a simple spreadsheet. When I say I'm not good at math, I mean I've never even learned my times tables. My parents moved our family from Chicago to Miami Beach when I was in the middle of the third grade and by the time I was resettled in my new elementary school, I'd fallen far behind. Building math skills is like build-ing blocks and because I'd missed a few in the move, I never did catch up. I struggled through middle and high school getting Ds in math. At some point I gave up trying to get any better. I felt liberated and such a sense of relief once I finally admitted to myself in my twenties that math just isn't my strength! (If I *had* been good at math, I'm sure I would have become an architect as it's a passion of mine.

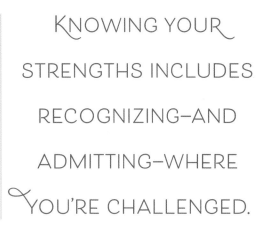

KNOWING YOUR STRENGTHS INCLUDES RECOGNIZING—AND ADMITTING—WHERE YOU'RE CHALLENGED.

But I let that dream go and built other dreams based on my strengths.)

Pat and I realized that we wouldn't be able to grow the company alone, relying only on our eye for design and people skills. So Pat and I approached SCORE (Ser-vice Corp of Retired Executives), a nationwide nonprofit that provides free busi-ness planning, financing, and marketing advice to entrepreneurs by matching them with retired executives. We were matched with an advisor, George Cook, an older gentleman who had had a great career in business. George was financially conservative, though, and my "ready, fire, aim" approach made him nervous, as did my lack of any real business training. Still, he took Pat and me under his wing and tirelessly taught us costing and pricing, among other business fundamen-tals. In his steady, quiet way, he encouraged us to "take it slow," and where we learned from him how to operate like a viable company, he also learned from us.

I remember George once scolding us over our phone bill. "Instead of making phone calls, he said, "you could send postcards to your buyers for a fraction of this cost."

"But, George." I laughed. "You have to *talk* to people. You have to build rela-tionships to build business. It's about more than numbers." Knowing this was *my* strength.

I have absolutely built Vera Bradley by embracing my God-given talents and doing more of what I do well. Where I am lacking or could use some extra help,

I'M IN AWE WHEN I MEET SOMEONE WITH TALENTS I'LL NEVER POSSESS. THIS GIVES ME STRENGTH.

I ask for support. Far from being an admission of inadequacy, this colorful collaboration of strengths and talents is what has allowed the company to grow to where it is today. I also apply this to working with people who have my strengths, but *stronger*. The day Vera Bradley hired fashion industry icon and Saks Fifth Avenue store designer Harry Cunningham to be our head of store development was one of my most thrilling. He brings such sophistication to all that he touches. We share a similar passion for and strength in design, but at times his talent surpasses mine. I love this. After working with Harry on our first project together, and also learning of our mutual love of Broadway, I opened our next executive meeting singing the musical hit "I'm Just Wild About Harry."

My attitude is that if someone can do it better than I can—have at it! I'm in awe when I meet someone with talents I'll never possess. This gives *me* strength.

GIVE *yourself* A BREAK

You don't have to be strong at everything. Be grateful for who you are and what you do well. Celebrate your unique strengths and appreciate the talents of others. What can you build on for your next redesign? And where you might need extra support, can you elicit the help of those who can share some of their strengths with you?

THE BEST IDEA WINS

I've always been fascinated by the audition process for the New York Philharmonic. From what I understand, the auditioning musicians play behind a curtain so they can't be physically identified. This allows the judges to hear the music without any visual distractions. (Think *The Voice*, but in black tie.) I imagine that as the music director hears each note rise and fall, he is listening acutely for the way each musician plays from his or her unique strength.

At Vera Bradley I similarly encourage everyone to play to his or her own tune and not be afraid to play *loudly*. We are a collaborative team where everyone has a voice, with ideas and opinions that deserve to be heard. I welcome other people's opinions and I expect everybody to have one.

Just because my title reads chief creative officer doesn't mean I have the final say. Whoever has the best idea wins. And a lot of the time the most junior members, or someone with a completely outside perspective, will have the best idea. That's why we positioned the design center in the middle of the building. It's here that we sketch out and choose fabrics for the next season of products, and it's here that we always welcome input. Whoever walks by—and this has included the UPS delivery man—may be asked for an opinion.

"What do you think of this pattern?"

"How does the length of this strap feel?"

"Would you want a bag with this many pockets?"

I remember we were designing a yoga sport bag when a woman who works in sales walked by and pointed out that the side straps should be adjustable to hold a yoga mat. What a brilliant detail! The employee noticed this, of course, because she practices yoga daily. The reality is that the design team can become so absorbed and engrossed in a product line that we can sometimes lose our objectivity, miss an important detail—or in my case overthink a design. (When I've looked at too many prints, I start seeing strange body parts, especially in paisley and floral. I blame my Catholic upbringing for this and it's become a bit of a joke in the design room. "Barb's seeing bodies again!") But seriously, you pick something apart long enough and you pick it apart.

At one point, we installed a floor-to-ceiling white board for anyone and everyone in the building to jot down ideas for print and product names. I encouraged people to throw anything and everything up on the wall. It might not stick. It might get cut. But every idea gets a look. After all, a bad idea can lead to a good idea and an even better idea. One season, a man working in the IT department named our best-selling fall print.

You see, there's really no room for hierarchy when it comes to ideas. In this business, I've been on every rung of the ladder and I know that an inspired thought can come from anyone and anywhere, so I encourage everyone to come to the table with an opinion and speak up. Some of our quieter new hires can be hesitant at first. The main reason, they've told me, is that they aren't accustomed to such an inclusive environment but over time they come to trust that the encouragement to have an

THERE'S REALLY NO ROOM FOR HIERARCHY WHEN IT COMES TO IDEAS.

individual voice is real and that's when they step forward and ask to be heard.

Around the Vera Bradley design table, I make a point of listening to every voice in the room, and I'm more than happy to be talked out of my own way of thinking. My feeling is that if someone hands me a better idea or a more colorful solution, I'll take it. I believe that remaining open to a variety of perspectives is how a company stays relevant and not locked into old patterns. At Vera Bradley, we invite everyone to help push the brand—to encourage us to think differently—to have that better idea. I said once to an incoming designer, "We didn't hire you to agree with us. We want to hear *your* ideas."

What I've discovered is that in business and in life, when you're willing to accept ideas from everyone around you and remain open to change, you get *so much more*. When people feel encouraged to express themselves and play from their individual strengths, they typically give their all. It's in an atmosphere of positive motivation where the best ideas enter the room.

WHEN YOU'RE WILLING TO ACCEPT IDEAS FROM EVERYONE AROUND YOU AND REMAIN OPEN TO CHANGE, YOU GET *SO MUCH MORE.*

BE *Open* TO THOSE AROUND YOU

I give as much freedom to my employees as I did to my own children. I was not a helicopter parent and I'm not a micromanager.

How are you at handing over control? Are you open to suggestions and willing to change your mind when someone around you has a better idea? It shouldn't matter whose idea it is. If it's the best one in the room, go with it.

DEFINE SUCCESS

Pat and I started Vera Bradley on the premise that we would create a product that brought us enjoyment and would also add color to the lives of other women. Truly, this was our single driving motivation. We didn't create our first duffel with the intention of making a lot of money, or even a little bit of money. Financial success wasn't our short- or even our long-term goal. Even today, the bottom line isn't my motivating force, though I'm sure our shareholders would like me to feel differently.

My eagerness to get into the office before nine o'clock every Monday morning isn't driven by the company's earnings or quarterly reports, but rather by the opportunity to continue to do creative work that both challenges and fulfills me, and to do it alongside people I consider family. That's the perfect way to earn a living, if you ask me. Find work that uplifts you. And only *you* can know what that is.

When my oldest grandson, Christopher, admitted to me that he "wasn't exactly passionate" about his business management degree or his finance internship, I

> FIND WORK THAT UPLIFTS YOU. AND ONLY YOU CAN KNOW WHAT THAT IS.

encouraged him to go back to school and discover that thing that did motivate him. "Someone else can work for Goldman Sachs," I reassured him. "It doesn't have to be you." It turns out that Christopher is much happier in the classroom because his strengths revolve around learning and leading. I'm so proud of him for honoring and pursuing his true calling. He's now a middle school teacher and basketball coach. And his students are lucky enough to be taught by someone who changed the direction of his life because of his love for teaching them.

Whenever anyone in the company wants to move on or change tracks, I encourage them wholeheartedly, as I did with Christopher. The last thing I want is an unhappy employee. I want everyone who works for Vera Bradley to be as excited as I am to get to the office every day. And if you're not, you have our full permission to find a work environment or a way to spend your time that does excite you. When Sue Britton, our vice president of marketing, came to me and said she was ready to move on and start her own marketing company, I encouraged her to do so. I wished her well and sent her off with a hug. And when six months later she launched her own marketing agency, we hired her to represent Vera Bradley. We were one of her first clients.

The truth is that some endeavors will be more successful and rewarding than others, which is why, throughout my life, I've challenged myself to keep moving forward no matter what the hurdle. Pat always joked that I'm like a car that doesn't have a brake pedal. My response: *Why stop? Why settle?* What I've come to believe—because it happened to me—is that when you partner perseverance with a faith in infinite possibilities, you cannot lose. You will find a way to succeed.

> WHEN YOU PARTNER PERSEVERANCE WITH A FAITH IN INFINITE POSSIBILITIES, YOU CANNOT LOSE. YOU WILL FIND A WAY TO SUCCEED.

I'm often asked why I still go into work every day. Some of my retired friends suggest that I slow down, smell the roses, and put my feet up. Ha! They should know better. I don't plan on putting my feet up anytime soon because I love what I do and I expect I'll continue to feel this way until the day I die. In fact, I plan for my retirement speech and eulogy to be one and the same. In the meantime—to those who want to sit back and relax, please go ahead. If you want to reach me, call me at the office.

DO WHAT YOU *Love*

Are you doing what you really love? If not, what's stopping you? Don't be afraid to change your path. No matter your age or where you are in your life, give yourself permission to do what you love—those things that make you eager to get back to it on Monday morning and every day of the week. There are infinite possibilities. Pursue whatever excites you.

KEEP THE ƒ IN FUN

I was making my closing comments at a company-wide sales meeting of nearly five hundred people when I ended with, "No matter what we're doing, we have to keep the *ƒ* in fun." Nearly everyone laughed because what they'd heard was, "We have to keep the *effin* fun," with an emphasis on the expletive! I laughed, too, but I didn't take back what I'd said. How could I, when my point was so colorfully made?

I've never considered my role at Vera Bradley "work" because I've had fun since day one. What's that familiar saying—*if you love your work, you'll never work a day in your life.* I believe in this wholeheartedly. The route to success has to be fun. If you're only in it for the end goal, and you're not having fun getting there, you're not really succeeding.

It's personal enjoyment that motivates me in everything I do—that, along with a desire to make people happy. Giving others a reason to smile drives all of my interactions, and also the direction of the Vera Bradley brand. The design team, for example, is always coming up with creative ways to delight the woman carrying our products. The intention of the patterned linings and many of the bright, interior colors in our bags, luggage, and accessories is meant to surprise

> FUN IS INTEGRAL TO CREATIVITY, PRODUCTIVITY, SUCCESS, AND LONG-TERM HAPPINESS.

whoever discovers it. We lined the inside of our calf-hair cheetah collection with a playful kitten pattern for no other reason *than for fun.*

When you make the extra effort to bring a smile to someone's face, they feel your attention and care. We've always said that at Vera Bradley we're creating more than a bag. We're creating good feelings and happy memories. To me, this is worth more than anything else.

When we sit around our design roundtable, I'm the senior voice (meaning I'm the oldest bag in the room), and yet when choosing new fabrics and styles, it's me, the seventy-something-year-old, who gravitates most toward whimsy while the younger designers often lean more conservative. I sometimes wonder if it shouldn't be the other way around. Maybe the younger girls haven't yet embraced what I've come to know so well: having fun every day is as important as brushing your teeth. Where I appreciate their attention to the business end of things, I'll sometimes interrupt a serious discussion on trend studies, for example, by saying, "Girls, these are handbags not defibrillators. Let's remember to have some fun."

Every day I look for opportunities for a good laugh (often at my own expense), and I learned this from my parents. They placed a high value on fun, and always infused our home with a strong sense of it. One of my fondest memories is of one evening when Dad came strolling through the living room in his swimming trunks. We were living in Miami Beach, where it can often feel too hot to wear much else. "The least you can do," Mother teased, "is get dressed for dinner." Thirty minutes later, Dad showed up in the dining room in a full tuxedo.

It might have been his influence that caused me, years later, to surprise some of my own dinner guests. I was throwing a party in New York for some business partners from Japan when, toward the end of the evening, I came marching into the living room in my tap shoes, twirling my baton. Dad used to say, in business

My father was a salesman

who made fun a part of every day.

Here he is with me and my sister Joan.

and in life, if you can make people laugh and also laugh at yourself, you'll get along just fine.

Having fun creates better collaboration and an overall sense of teamwork and we plan all of our company events with fun in mind. After several years of leading the charge (which I literally once did when after putting up a new flagpole I blasted marching music throughout the office and encouraged everyone to follow in line), we created an official "Happy Committee" to encourage an overall sense of playfulness at Vera Bradley. Pat and I realized that if we continued to plan all the company events, they'd all be the same. But if we gave other people the opportunity to host, the potential for even more fun would multiply.

Today, our Happy Committee has their own budget to plan regular events that inspire fun, such as: bowling, brunch, and barbeques. Really, it can be anything. Back when the company was exclusively female, except for one gentleman named Bob who worked in our distribution center, the committee enacted "Bob Day," where once a year we dedicated the day to our lone man by dressing in ball caps and plaid shirts. We did silly things like "bobbing" for apples in the break room and eating birthday cake that said HAPPY BOB DAY!

Over the years I've been told by enough people who have worked at other companies that the culture at Vera Bradley is not how most other corporate environments are run, let alone reflected in the attitudes of those who run them. A friend and colleague of mine said she once worked for a company that she was sure must have had a "Misery Committee." "How else could they have encouraged such gloom?" she wondered. I laughed when I heard this, and then recognized this might not have been the most appropriate response to my friend's unhappy memory. But, really, a workplace that gloomy, I cannot imagine! I'm happy to report that, at age fifty, she found a new and much better job where she is thriving today. Talk about a redesign!

Not long after hiring Harry Cunningham, he said, "I worked for Saks for nearly twenty years. Barb, things are very different here. Everyone who works at Vera Bradley acts like they're hooked up to happy gas."

"Good," I responded. "That's exactly how I want it."

We set high expectations for productivity and we also expect people to have fun. Are people happy and content? Is the mood playful, as well as productive? As long as the answer is yes, I feel we're running a successful company. I have to think that the reason our voluntary turnover rate is close to zero has something to do with our emphasis on keeping the *effin* fun.

I was once asked to speak at the Drexel Heritage Furniture headquarters in North Carolina, where we were introducing a collaboration between our two companies. The collection was splashy, with vibrant colors and bold patterns at a time when the interiors market was predominantly beige. In the audience were various design and style experts, including magazine editors from the top publications around the country. When it was my turn to take the podium I decided not to speak just about the collection, but about the Vera Bradley culture. Imagine the surprise when I told this very sophisticated group of New Yorkers about our Happy Committee. I explained that the committee helps plan ice-cream socials, shopping trips to Chicago, and a monthly supper club. I also mentioned the surprise gifts employees often find on their desks. *Just for fun.*

At the end of my talk, what do you think happened?

Did the super-chic, maybe even jaded visitors from New York shun our small Midwestern company?

No. I was mobbed.

Reporters in the crowd wanted to know more. *What a great idea!* Business leaders said, *I want this for my company!* They asked me for ideas on how to create their own Happy Committees. When I later joined a Vera Bradley colleague after the event, we both laughed. "No matter where you're from," I said, "girls just want to have fun."

Every day I look for ways to keep the *f* in fun, and sometimes this means making your own. A perfect example of this is when Kim Colby, our colleague, and I

I BELIEVE THAT GIRLS REALLY DO JUST WANT TO HAVE FUN. AND A REWARDING LIFE, TOO!

once took a trip to our primary printing mill in North Carolina. We only expected to be there for a day to watch the fabric being printed, as well as check color and print registration, but there were complications and so we ended up staying for four days.

We'd spent every day at the mill working late into the evening and on the morning of the fourth day, I looked at Kim as she was getting dressed in the same clothes she'd worn every day since arriving.

I said, "I cannot look at you in those clothes anymore and you're probably sick of looking at me. Take them off and give yours to me, and you can wear mine."

That morning we switched outfits and everyone at the mill got a great kick when we showed up dressed as each other.

Later that same evening, as Kim and I were grabbing a bite at the hotel restaurant, my husband Peer called looking for me. This was before cell phones, you see, so he called the front desk receptionist and asked if she'd look for me in the dining room.

"What does she look like?" the receptionist asked.

Peer gave his automatic response. "She's a cute redhead."

Well, after four days in the same clothes and without a hair dryer and probably looking like death warmed over, I'm sure I didn't look too cute. A minute later, when the receptionist returned to the phone she confidently reported to Peer, "She's not here."

Kim and I laugh over this story to this day because we *had* been in the restaurant. We didn't look cute, but we were sure having fun.

ARE YOU HAVING *Fun* YET?

Fun is magic medicine. It will improve your life, if not extend it. So ask yourself how much fun you're having from day to day. There's always room for more, so prescribe yourself an extra dose and then notice how your life and work start to feel a whole lot better. Not having any fun? Then take this as your cue: consider a change, *now*.

SLIP UP FROM TIME TO TIME

Several years ago I was invited to Japan to launch a Vera Bradley store within Isetan, the most prestigious department store in Tokyo. While there, I was asked if I would speak to a group of Isetan's top female customers about starting Vera Bradley. Female entrepreneurs, and especially self-made ones, are few and far between in Japan, so I felt honored for the opportunity to tell my story, and took my position seriously.

The day of the private luncheon, I stepped onto a small platform stage and addressed the reserved, impeccably dressed, and elegant crowd. With a microphone in one hand and an interpreter by my side, I began talking about how we'd started the company with just five hundred dollars we'd borrowed from our husbands, and how we can each find ways to lead more colorful lives. Well, not even five minutes into my talk, I felt something fall down my legs. I looked down, and to my alarm saw that my half-slip was bunched up around my ankles.

MISTAKES ARE REAL AND WHEN YOU MAKE THEM, PEOPLE WILL RELATE TO YOUR AUTHENTICITY.

Oh shit, I said to myself. And then—*thank goodness I'd worn a nice one!* The women noticed it, too. Some of them gasped while others shyly giggled and looked around the crowd as I decided what to do next. There was really no dignified way out of this. I wasn't going to pull it back up, so I thought, *let's have some fun.* I stepped out of my slip, picked it up off of the floor, and swung it over my head.

"I bet you ladies didn't think you were coming for a strip show!" I told them.

I'm not sure how the interpreter translated this, but the crowd erupted into laughter and applause. It was not unlike the time movie star Jennifer Lawrence tripped onstage before her 2013 acceptance speech for best actress in *Silver Linings Playbook.* She endeared herself to us in that moment for revealing what we all are—imperfect and human. My unintentional slipup (or slip *down*) had instantly made me more relatable as a real woman who sometimes loses her skirt, and this disclosure instantly connected me to everyone in the room.

We're all friends now, I thought to myself as I collected my slip. And indeed, the formal event took a turn toward playful. At the end of the luncheon one of Isetan's top customers walked up to me and put her finger to her lips. She whispered in clear English, "This never happened." We both laughed, but in truth, I was happy that it had. It taught me a valuable lesson—mistakes are real and when you make them, people will relate to your authenticity.

I often think back to my slipup moment in Japan when I give any speech or have to address a crowd. I'm reminded to just be me. To speak carefully—but not too carefully. In my experience this is who people really want to meet—the real person.

I regularly travel the country speaking to college students, women's organizations, colleagues in the gift industry, and others in business. Knowing what I've learned, I hardly ever prepare for speeches. No notes. No index cards. I understand that an unscripted speech doesn't work for everybody. Most people are fearful of public speaking (sometimes deathly!), but the truth is that the crowd will have already embraced you before you've even said your first word for simply having the courage to get onstage. Then, when you reveal yourself as someone real and relatable, you'll win them over completely.

I think it was the third year we exhibited at the Chicago gift show that we realized during setup that we didn't have enough Vera Bradley samples to show in the booth. We'd brought as much as we could pack into our van and we'd also shipped boxes of product up with the cabinets, tables, and extras to create a homey feel in our booth. But once we'd unpacked and displayed it all, we saw that we needed more bags. So I drove back to the Whitehall Hotel to grab our own personal Vera Bradley duffels and totes so that we'd have enough inventory to fill the booth.

I remember dumping out my sister Joan's neatly packed bag followed by my own, which was not at all organized. (I've never been that kind of packer—probably why we first designed duffels because you can just throw everything in one!)

Well, five days later when the show ended, we automatically packed most everything up in boxes to be shipped back to Fort Wayne. When we returned to the hotel it dawned on us. We'd packed up our personal luggage and now had nothing to put our clothes and toiletries in. We were the luggage ladies with no luggage! That night, we stuffed all of our personal belongings into the hotel pillowcases. When we checked out the next morning with stuffed linens in hand, I told the receptionist that we'd lost our luggage and asked if I could please pay her for the bedding. She smiled at the comedy of it and offered us a friendly solution—take them home and send them back.

JUST BE YOU. THIS IS WHAT PEOPLE REALLY WANT TO SEE—THE REAL PERSON.

Slips HAPPEN

Let go of your fear of making a mistake because, from time to time, slips happen to everyone. They're what make us real. How might you redefine or even reinvent yourself by being *more of yourself*?

IT'S GOOD
TO BE A GIRL

In my professional and personal life, I have a reputation for saying and often doing the unexpected. My colleague Kim Colby says about me, "Barb has no problem taking the conversation south." It's true that there aren't many words that I won't use if the situation calls for it. Sometimes you have to let a few inappropriate words fly to make your point.

In 2015 I was a guest speaker at Tory Johnson's Women for Hire and Spark & Hustle conference about the advantages of being a woman in business. Tory's annual conferences of up to eight thousand people deliver actionable advice and ideas for women and men who value personal and professional development. When asked by a woman in the audience what it was like when our all-female company brought in men at the executive level, I said, "The strong feminine culture did shift when the company started hiring more men. Almost overnight," I continued, "it became the chicks versus the dicks."

As soon as it came out of my mouth, I thought, *Oops, did I just say that out loud?* The crowd erupted in laughter and later, according to the head of Tory's

> WOMEN ARE STRONGER TOGETHER. WE NATURALLY WORK BEST AS A COLLABORATIVE FORCE.

social media department, it was one of the more "Tweetable" quotes of the day. Imagine that—a seventy-something-year-old woman trending on Twitter!

While I realized what I'd said was funny because of its shock value, I hadn't meant to imply that introducing men to the company had created a gender war. It hadn't. I told them that I'd never felt like being a woman was a disadvantage or had hindered me in business. In fact, I think it's served as an advantage because I'm a woman designing for women. I understand my customer's perspective because I *am* her. I know what she wants because I want it for myself.

What I'd actually meant by my "us versus them" comment was that the new male hires didn't seem as accustomed to our family culture. Women instinctively know how to build families, which, in my opinion, is exactly what you're doing when you form a company. Pat and I hired our best girlfriends, sisters, and nieces as the first sales reps and we've been adding women to the family ever since. Being a company of women has always been one of our strongest points because women are stronger together. We naturally work best as a collaborative force. At Vera Bradley, we use "we" more than "I." Everything we make and create, we've done together. The swapping and sharing of ideas, insights, and inspiration that tends to easily flow between women is the foundation of our creative culture, so when the company started hiring more men, the environment didn't become gender divided and competitive necessarily; the men simply took a different approach.

I noticed, for example, an almost automatic proclivity by the men in the group to offer advice, rather than participate in the volley of ideas. This is an important distinction. Again, I'll accept input from everyone at the table, and while I regarded many of the male voices in the room as trying to be helpful (and Vera Bradley has been helped by many generous men along the way), there came a point when we had to make the point: being a man doesn't give you any more power around here. The best idea wins, regardless of gender, race, age, or whatever else. And at the end of the day, we applaud teamwork over individual success.

Sue Fuller, our chief merchandising officer, likes to tell the story of her first day at Vera Bradley. I stopped by her office and said, "I'm so glad you're here. I hope we don't ever disappoint you."

She expressed to me later how much those words affected her. She was accustomed to her employers setting an expectation from the start that she not disappoint them. And here I'd turned it around. I'd put the emphasis on us. She wanted to know why.

I said, "Because we're in this together."

Sue smiled. She totally got it. Of course she did. She's a girl.

WHO'S ON *Your* TEAM?

In what areas of your life can you be a bigger part of the team? We all have ideas and insights to share, with none better than another, based on gender, age, or race. So step forward and make sure yours are heard and in exchange, respectfully consider the voices around you.

KNOW YOUR AUDIENCE

It's true that I surprise people when I speak in "inappropriate" sound bites, but I was taught by my mother and father to speak my mind and to have a sense of humor whenever possible. Of course, you have to know how to read the room. When my granddaughter Frannie was in the third grade, I was asked to speak to her class about entrepreneurship. I thought the topic was a bit above the heads of this four-foot-tall audience, but I accepted the invitation.

The day of the event, I took my place in front of twenty or so third graders and began telling them about how I started Vera Bradley and how they someday might have a business idea of their own. I'd come up with five business "tips" I thought they might understand and as I went through them, I could see their eyes glazing over at the mention of "how to build a cottage industry with friends" and "it's important to make a product that people want." One by one, I was losing them.

So, I quickly shifted my focus.

"Enough about business. How about I talk about Frannie and the day she was born?" I said.

KNOW YOUR AUDIENCE, AND ONLY GIVE THEM WHAT THEY WANT TO HEAR

The children perked up, so I continued.

"It was December thirty-first, New Year's Eve, which was my husband Peer's birthday. We planned to go out for a fancy dinner to celebrate, but just as we were heading out the door to the restaurant, we received a call from Frannie's daddy who told us that Frannie's mommy was in the hospital. She was getting ready to have her baby."

Frannie's class all looked at Frannie and then back at me with their full attention.

"Well, this was before cell phones, so Peer and I decided to stay in and make ourselves comfortable while we waited by the phone. You see, I didn't want to miss hearing when my grandchild was born. So we waited and waited until it got so late that Peer said he was sleepy and ready for bed. I gave him a kiss goodnight and continued to wait for the phone to ring and finally, not long after hearing midnight bells ringing in the New Year, I received a call that Frannie had been born! It was New Year's Day."

Frannie's classmates clapped with delight, and that was the end of my introduction to entrepreneurship for third graders.

About a week later, I began receiving cards in the mail. They were from Frannie's classmates. "Dear Mrs. Baekgaard," they said, "thank you for coming to our class . . . but we are so sad Peer missed his birthday." Nearly all the cards shared a similar sentiment. They'd drawn little birthday cakes in crayon with tears and sad faces next to them that said, "Poor Peer didn't get his party," and "We're sad he didn't get a birthday cake."

I couldn't help laughing. The only thing they'd retained of my business tips was this story about Peer. The lesson: know your audience, and only give them what they want to hear.

Me, with nine of my grandchildren in 2001.

WHO'S *Your* AUDIENCE?

Whose attention do you want to get? Whether it's another individual, a large company, or a classroom of children, craft your message specifically for them. Speak to them in their language. When you know your audience, it's much easier to know exactly what to say and do.

Color
Your
Relationships

CHOOSE NICE

A reporter once asked me about the practice Vera Bradley sales reps have of sending personal, handwritten notes to our affiliates and partners. "Do you teach your employees to write thank-you notes?" the reporter asked. "I don't have to," I replied. "At Vera Bradley, we don't teach nice—*we hire nice*." In fact, nice people are the only ones who get through the front door.

One of Dad's favorite songs was "Never Met a Man I Didn't Like" from the Will Rogers Follies. An oldie but a goodie, the song starts out with all the different people Will Rogers has met—the prince of Wales, a working joe, a false evangelist—then goes on to say that some of them would have made him change his mind were it not for that certain touch that humans have, that capacity for understanding what makes another person what he is. It's a "walk a mile in my shoes" type of song, and it really suited Ed Bradley to a T.

Dad had a generous and welcoming spirit that he imparted to us. I really do believe that it's important to look at things from other people's perspective. Nevertheless, while I generally like about 90 percent of the people I meet, I also have a fairly strict— *ahem*— "no asshole" policy. While my short list is short, once

BE INTERESTED RATHER THAN INTERESTING.

you're on it, you're out. One of my colleagues jokes that I'd be great at speed dating because I can weed out the less desirable candidates quickly. It's true, I can. And it's partly due to my "dinner test." When I first meet someone, I ask myself, *Would I like to have dinner with this person?* If the answer is yes—great! If the answer is no, then I probably don't want to do business with them, either.

I once attended a dinner party where I sat next to a man who struck up a conversation with me—all about himself! Throughout the first course and into the second, he wouldn't stop talking about his work . . . his interests . . . his life. If that weren't distasteful enough, he also needled me to play silly games like, "let's only eat with our left hands" or "let's use our spoons instead of our forks." I love getting silly, but in the case of my dinner companion, it was clear to me that he felt that he was the most interesting guest at the table and could modify our hostess's dinner plans as he wished. In his zeal to break with the perfectly fine tradition of enjoying the beautiful table she'd set, the food she'd carefully chosen, and the friends she'd thoughtfully put together, he was also breaking another one of my tried and true relationship rules—*be interested rather than interesting.* Indeed, he acted like I'd landed the jackpot to have his attention for the night. After the coffee and dessert dishes were cleared, I finally turned to him and said, "I have a game we can play." His ears perked up like a puppy anticipating an after-dinner treat. "How about you tell me everything you've learned about *me* tonight and I'll tell you everything I know about you."

Who do you think won that game?

Sometimes, you get stuck in situations where you can't just get up from the table and leave. And to my mind, it's better to take the high road and be gracious, rather than dismissive or unkind. In situations where I may be rubbed the wrong way by another person's comment or behavior, I make a concerted effort to just let people *be.* Every person can think and act as he or she wants. What is the point of trying to convert another person's opinions or actions? It hardly ever works. What *does* seem to work is to counter the negative with the positive. It's a conscious choice I make every day to be positive and to surround myself, as much as I can, with people who support and even uplift me. I believe we can all make a similar choice.

With my children,

who support and uplift me every day. 1974.

THE *Company* YOU KEEP

Are you surrounded by people in your life who uplift you? Take notice of the people in your day-to-day life. How do they behave toward you and those around you? How do you feel in their company? A happy home or work environment is contingent on surrounding yourself with people you like and respect enough to share a meal with. In the Midwest, we call these "the good people."

TITLES MEAN (ALMOST) NOTHING

Your next wonderful work environment is contingent on working with people you like enough to share a meal with. I believe this so strongly that I'll often rely on my "dinner test" even before I read someone's resume.

In my experience, resumes are often unreliable; they don't tend to tell the whole story of who someone is, never mind the true range of their interests and abilities. I feel the same way about job titles. When recently I was asked who Vera Bradley's senior director of product development is, I replied quite honestly, "I'm not sure we even have one."

Nearly four hundred people work in the Vera Bradley design center, and I recognize you all and make a point to call you by name. But I won't always remember your job title and I don't apologize for that. I hope I don't offend anyone, but I know I'd rather be called Barb than the chief creative officer; and I just cringe when anyone refers to me as "the boss." (At Vera Bradley we say that we work *with* someone, not *for* someone.)

I believe that you are more than your job title. Your contribution extends well beyond a list of bullet points. Labels and titles are just words on paper and don't accurately reflect a person's true personality. They don't communicate the feeling you get when you sit across from someone at the dinner table or speak privately on the phone. My feelings tell me much more than a list of credentials on nice paper stock, so I like to meet someone before I review his or her resume. Of course, I do have some help. By the time any candidate for employment sits down with me, I know that others have already reviewed their application, including my executive assistant, Debbie Wilson.

We hired Debbie as a temporary receptionist twenty-two years ago, and it didn't take long before I recognized how valuable she was. Meticulous and articulate, Debbie could manage a calendar like a world-class juggler. Plus, she instinctively knew how to prioritize and screen calls coming into the office. "It's your son Jimmy on line one; he says it's not too important. I've asked him to call back." "It's Leo Driscoll from VIP Fabrics. I'm going to put him through." Almost instantly, I knew I could trust her natural inclinations and judgment. She saved me a lot of time doing the thinking for me and I knew that I couldn't let her go. I feel strongly that when you find valuable people, you find a way to keep them in your life. I offered Debbie a full-time job as my personal assistant as quickly as I could.

Today, if you were to ask anyone in my family, they'd say Debbie is much more than her title. She's one of my closest allies. My wingwoman. Not only do I rely on her to review most employment applications for me (and remind me of people's job titles), I also rely on her to provide me with her impression of the person I'm about to be introduced to. Remember: I only hire nice, and I expect that anyone coming to meet the head of the company will put on their nicest face. The true test of a person's character shows through in the way

> YOU ARE MORE THAN YOUR JOB TITLE. YOUR CONTRIBUTION EXTENDS WELL BEYOND A LIST OF BULLET POINTS.

they behave toward the people they interact with before me. "How were you treated?" I'll ask Debbie. "Was he respectful to you on the phone? Was she friendly? Was he gracious to the driver who picked him up at the airport?" Once I asked Debbie about a candidate for a top management position. "What did you think of him?" Before I even got the full sentence out, she gave me The Look that meant

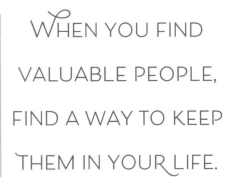

WHEN YOU FIND VALUABLE PEOPLE, FIND A WAY TO KEEP THEM IN YOUR LIFE.

flatly, *no*. She said she knew it the moment he walked through the door by the way he muttered a "hello" without making eye contact. "It was as if he couldn't be bothered," she said. That was all I needed to hear. He didn't get hired.

We are a culture-first company so that means finding people who are a match, and not everybody is. I liken it to picking the right sorority. If you aren't a fit for the Alpha Sigma Kappas, perhaps you can find a home with the Delta Gammas. What's most important is identifying what type of culture is the best fit for *you*.

Nice: THE BEST FOUR-LETTER WORD

Follow your heart and your instincts when choosing whom you surround yourself with. Life is too short to spend time with people you don't enjoy or respect. If the people around you each day aren't your version of "nice," and don't match how you wish your environment could be, consider this yet another reason for making a change in your life.

INVITE CONNECTION

O nce when I was shopping at L.K.Bennett in New York, I was so impressed with how helpful and honest the sales clerk was that before I left the store, I asked for her card. Turns out, she was the store manager. Once out on the street I turned to my friend Glenna and said, "She would be perfect for Vera Bradley." When I returned to the Fort Wayne corporate office, I handed her card to Melissa, our head of retail stores, and suggested that the next time she was recruiting for store managers, she might contact this woman. Well not two months later, Melissa appeared in my office doorway. "Barb, you won't believe who I just hired to manage our new store opening in SoHo." Out of hundreds of candidates, she'd offered the job to the woman from L.K.Bennett. "She was everyone's top pick," Melissa said. "She fits in perfectly with Vera Bradley,"

In a way, I'm always recruiting people who are a fit for our unique culture, and if I feel a genuine connection with someone, I may hire them on the spot. My feeling is that you know when a relationship is wrong and you also know when it's right, which is exactly what happened when I hired Kim Colby nearly thirty years ago. Kim had read a tiny article about Pat and me in the *Indianapolis Business*

YOU KNOW WHEN A RELATIONSHIP IS WRONG AND YOU ALSO KNOW WHEN IT'S RIGHT.

Journal. She later told us that our story struck her as the perfect example of two women living the American dream, so when her husband's business brought her to Fort Wayne she decided to drop by our office and introduce herself.

My daughter Amy was working as the receptionist that day and she buzzed me. "A Kim Colby wants to say hello."

Kim had great style, and carried a brand of spunk I recognized in myself, so of course I liked her instantly. But for at least the first fifteen minutes of our time together I continued to mistakenly call her Lynn until she politely corrected me, "It's Kim. I worked at the firm Lynn Hummer."

We laughed at my mix-up and talked more about her design background. Finally she said, "You know, I'd love to work *here.*"

At the time, Vera Bradley was still young and we weren't necessarily in a financial position to hire more employees, but I asked her anyway, "What do you want to do?"

"I don't know," she admitted. "Anything! I'm just so in love with what you're building here—real women designing for real women. I want to be part of it."

"Just a minute," I said. I took her résumé into Pat's office and said, "We have to hire this girl. She said she'd do *anything.*"

And that was the day we offered Kim a position at Vera Bradley. She's been with the company for nearly three decades now. She has a big title, if only I could remember what it is.

If I want to hire someone I may have to find or even create a position at the company regardless of whether or not there is an opening to fill or if his or her credentials are a perfect match. I'm a nightmare for human resources in this way. I'll go in and say, "I want to hire so-and-so. She's a forty-five-year-old mother of four, grew up in Chicago, and is recently remarried to a man who's widowed."

"How do you know all that?" Julie North, our head of HR will say.

"I asked her."

Julie will inevitably shake her head and drop it into her hands. "Barbara, you cannot ask personal questions like that."

Julie's been with the company since we were only sixty-five employees and now we're over three thousand company wide. She won't even sit in the room with me when I interview an applicant because my line of questioning often crosses it.

I can't help it.

I don't *want* to help it.

I want to know where someone grew up, how many siblings they have, if they've traveled, and how they met their best friend. All of these factors paint the picture of a person, and I find people genuinely interesting. Once I interviewed a woman who told me that her daughter worked as an undertaker at a funeral home.

Naturally, I said, "Tell me more." And thus she became part of the Vera Bradley family.

My interviews are more like conversations because I invite people to tell me their personal story. I want to get to know the entire person, the full 360 view. What I've learned is that when you treat people with curiosity, kindness, and respect, you learn wonderful things about them. When we opened our Hong Kong office, I flew over from New York with a few others on the Vera Bradley management team including my daughter and my son-in-law, to meet the staff. I wanted to communicate to them that we hadn't just opened a satellite office. Despite our geographical distance, we were all part of the same team.

Prior to our arrival, we'd encouraged them to bring in pictures of their families, and when we all sat down

NOTHING CONVEYS INTEREST MORE THAN "TELL ME MORE."

together, I looked through their personal photos and asked them to tell me more about themselves. They regarded me dubiously. *Weren't we there to talk about business?* Once they realized that I'd flown over with members of my own family with the express purpose of getting to know them and theirs, they were overtly grateful. Contrary to how the Asian culture is often depicted as keeping a friendly distance, I received a lot of hugs in our Hong Kong office that day.

I received a similar reaction when I interviewed a candidate for our top management team 30,000 feet in the air on a plane from New York to Fort Wayne. Soon after we offered her the job, she said she couldn't believe that *that* had been our interview. "We didn't even talk about business." She laughed.

I told her, "I already knew enough about your professional background. I wanted to get to know *you*."

MAKING THE *Connection*

People do and give their best when they are encouraged to be more of who they really are. In what ways can you better connect to the people around you and get to know the full person? In my experience, the best connections are made when you pull curiosity and genuine interest out of your bag.

BE A FRIEND, MAKE A FRIEND

In taking the time to get to know someone and be interested in them, you add color and texture to your relationships. You create meaningful connections. I extend this to people from every corner of my life—my coworkers, grandchildren, friends, and even the young man who takes my coffee order at the Starbucks down the street. They all share with me interesting and often very personal details of their lives. Why? *Because I care enough to ask.* My practice is to treat everyone like they are important and interesting, because they are. And when you treat people like gold, they *feel it.*

A few years ago, *The New York Times* called me and explained they were doing a story on the building I live in when I'm working in New York. They wanted to know what was so special about living there and one of the first things I said was, "The staff. They're incredible." Well, about a month after the article appeared, several people who work in the building, including the doorman and the concierge approached me. They each thanked me for giving them recognition in such a public way. "Of course," I said and then thought to myself, *Why wouldn't*

WHEN YOU TREAT PEOPLE LIKE GOLD, THEY *FEEL* IT.

I? To describe the building without the people who make it what it is would have been an incredible oversight. I'm so appreciative of them, and I feel the same way about our Vera Bradley employees. Whenever I'm asked to give tours of the corporate headquarters, I do so *only* during the workday when everyone is there. In my opinion, the company only exists because of the people. Without them, it's just an empty facility, and that's how I regard the building I live in in New York.

Compare this with the experience of Walter Bettinger, president and CEO of Charles Schwab. Always an A student, he shared his feelings of embarrassment in an article I read about how he had failed his final exam in business school when he couldn't answer the question: *What is the name of the lady who cleans this building?* He didn't know the answer and he failed the test. He said, "I deserved that. I had seen her but never asked her name."

Her name was Dottie, and what a shame that he missed the opportunity to get to know her. Who knows how else he may have enriched his life beyond passing the simple test?

About fifteen years ago, on an ordinary day, my son-in-law Mike Ray flagged down a driver outside our hotel in Manhattan. The man who pulled over was named Gregory Philpotts and it happened to be his first day on the job. He'd recently moved to New York City from Jamaica and after only driving a few city blocks together, Mike and I were so charmed by him and his life story that we took his cell phone number and called him for another pickup later that day. Would you believe that from that day forward, Gregory became the one and only driver we called when we were in New York City? Over time, Gregory became so familiar with my life and I with his (you can really cover a lot of personal history while stuck in rush-hour traffic in Midtown), that before we realized it had happened, our lives were intertwined. I'll never forget the time he dropped me at a friend's birthday party. I'd meant to quickly run in and leave a gift, so I'd asked him to wait for me. More than an hour later, I felt terrible when I slid back into his car. I handed him a piece of cake as an apology.

"That's it?" he said. "You've been in there carrying on and all you bring me is a piece of cake? I'm starving out here. Where are the ribs?"

I laughed out loud, and I realized in that moment that Gregory had become much more than my driver. We were friends and our relationship extended well beyond business and hospitality. The next time I asked him to drive me to a party, I invited him in.

Years later, when my late husband, Peer, became sick and was no longer able to drive on his own, Gregory offered to temporarily move from New York to Fort Wayne to drive Peer wherever he needed to go. I wasn't too surprised that Gregory wanted to help Peer in whatever way he could; over the years, they had formed a friendship, too. Both immigrants, Peer and Gregory had probably spent hundreds of hours in the car discussing their love for this country and all the opportunities it had afforded them. Still, I was moved by Gregory's kindness and devotion toward my husband. I had not asked him to move to Fort Wayne. The decision was all his. When Peer passed away a year later, Gregory and his wife, Carolyn, attended the funeral alongside the rest of our family because that is what he'd become—one of us.

In my experience, one of the most powerful ways to add color to your life is by making connections. And we can each begin to do more of this by simply putting down our digital devices, looking people in the eye, and saying "Hello." It really is that simple. That's how I meet people every day in my life. I make a connection through eye contact, a friendly handshake, or by noticing some detail that I can be curious and ask about.

EVERY FRIENDSHIP STARTS WITH HELLO.

In the Midwest, where I'm from, these types of exchanges come easy because it's the Midwestern way. But in Manhattan, where I now spend a significant amount of my time, it takes a bit more effort to connect with people. Still, it can be done! For example, when I get into an elevator in New York, I make a point to say hello. When it comes to making a connection, someone has to go first and I'm fine that it's usually me. After that single-word hello, which could be anywhere—standing in line for coffee, waiting at your departure gate, or in the backseat of your Uber car—there's often some common thread to talk about—the weather, the news of the day, or the latest trend in handbags. Now, I'm not implying that you make conversation with everyone with whom you cross paths. My point is that making connections and even real friendships can happen anywhere you are when you decide to make the effort.

A FRIEND *Indeed*

"The only way to have a friend is to be one," said Ralph Waldo Emerson. When you treat everyone you meet as you would a friend, the world becomes a lot friendlier—on the street, in the boardroom, in the classroom, and wherever your life takes you. Are you creating connections wherever you go? It can happen with one word: hello. Simple introductions can become lasting friendships.

PRACTICE KINDNESS

Extending kindness and taking an interest in people is an act of generosity that I learned at an early age from my parents. It's such an automatic habit now that I don't think much about it. To be honest, I don't set out every day to be kind and generous. I just treat people how I want to be treated and this seems to serve me quite well in business and all other aspects of my life. Peer used to say, "We really don't need all ten commandments if everyone would just follow the Golden Rule."

I learned most things by watching the action unfold in my home growing up; the doors were always open to friends of friends of friends. Mother and Dad embraced a "the more the merrier" attitude. The way that Vera and Ed treated the people in their lives instilled a generosity in all of us. One of the most notable examples of this is by how they treated my brother Jamie.

My younger brother Jamie was born with cerebral palsy. He never developed beyond the level of a four-month-old; he couldn't sit, speak, or even roll over. As Mother used to tell the story, "It was accepted practice in those days to institutionalize children like Jamie." But Mother refused. She was fiercely adamant that

Jamie never leave our family or our home. Her message was clear to anyone who questioned her: this child is no less deserving of our love, care, attention, and commitment.

When Jamie turned two, we moved from the harsh winters of Chicago to Miami Beach. Mother believed that a warmer climate would make it easier to care for him and would also make the whole family more comfortable. She had a lovely upholstered swing designed for Jamie that hung from the ceiling of our large family room. It was more truly a hanging twin bed, where Jamie could be gently rocked by any and all of us throughout the day.

Jamie was always in our midst, and Mother designed it that way. She did not shamefully hide him upstairs, disguise or make excuses for his limitations and inabilities, but rather she presented him proudly to anyone who came through our front door. Mother continued to entertain as she always had—regular cocktail and dinner parties—and Jamie was included in our lively family atmosphere. I have many memories of Mother sitting next to Jamie on his swing, rubbing his arm or running her fingers through his beautiful red hair. He recognized voices and smiled to the touch and would gaze up at Mother happily while she engaged with whomever was in the room. Throughout my adolescent and teenage years, I took my cues from Mother. I'd proudly bring my friends home from school and introduce them to Jamie just as I did to my other four siblings. Mother encouraged us, "If you're just going to sit up and talk, go into Jamie's room so he can listen in." So that's what we did. My friends and I sat with Jamie on his swing as we talked the evening away. There was never any question, in my mind, that Jamie was one of us.

When I was eight years old, Vera realized that she needed help raising six children, including one with special needs. She placed an ad in the *Miami Herald*: "Woman wanted to live with a loving family and care for a special child." Not a day later, she received a phone call from a woman named Violet Pressnail. Violet explained that she was visiting her daughter from Toronto, Canada, but the ad had caught her attention. She couldn't get it off her mind. She asked, "Can I come out and meet you?" Violet took a bus to our home the next afternoon and didn't leave for fifteen years. She stayed by Jamie's side until the day he died.

My sister Joan and I nicknamed her "Pressie" and that is how she came to be called by everyone who met her. Mother set up a lovely room for her downstairs, but during her first night in our house a crashing thunderstorm woke her up. Pressie crawled out of bed and crept upstairs to Jamie's room. She curled up beside him to comfort him from the noise, and that's where she slept for the next fifteen years. Pressie was nearly always by Jamie's side and when she wasn't, he'd noticeably perk up and smile when he heard Pressie's voice or smelled her favorite Yardley perfume. It was startling and equally extraordinary to watch this slight woman who barely reached five feet and weighed no more than ninety pounds care for and lift my brother every day of his life. After converting to Catholicism and getting her American citizenship, she liked to joke that the only thing she couldn't do to become more like us was grow taller. But that didn't matter. Her actual height was insignificant in comparison to her generous spirit that loomed large in our family, demonstrating to us daily what it means to live with an open heart and outstretched arms.

When he was seventeen, Jamie developed pneumonia. After a brief stay in the hospital, Mother brought him home where he died quietly in her and Pressie's arms. Vera insisted that we all wear white to the funeral because "our sweet Jamie," she said, "has gone straight to heaven." He was buried in his pajamas and we all remarked how he looked to be sleeping peacefully.

Years later, I was out with Mother when we ran into Cher Bond, a woman who works at Vera Bradley. Cher was with her mother, Arlene, and her Down's syndrome younger brother, John. Vera had never met Cher's family and after being introduced she turned to Arlene. "Aren't you lucky," she said. "Our Jamie could never walk or talk and here you are"—she smiled at John—"growing up so handsome and strong." The next day at the office, Cher confided in me how touched she'd been by Mother's reaction. "No one ever looks at John, or our family, that way. They pity us for what we appear to be lacking."

I hadn't been surprised by Mother's reaction. It was just her way. And it became mine, too.

I believe that when you witness generosity and kindness of this caliber, it's impossible to be any other way. In other words, what we teach our children is important to us will become important to them. This translates to employees, too. From the very beginning, I've run Vera Bradley like a family and a household rather than a corporation. I set the same values, standards, and expectations in the workplace that I grew up with and what I later instilled in my own home.

LET *Kindness* BE YOUR WAY

What experiences in your own life have allowed you to be more caring, generous, and compassionate toward other people? Who have you met who's inspired you to reach out with greater love and kindness? Most of us are blessed by knowing at least one special person who encourages and empowers us to be our best self. For me, it was Vera. Who is it for you? And how can you be that person for someone else?

OPEN DOORS

I have an open-door policy wherever I'm working. To me, an open door says: *I want to be involved. I invite you in.*

At the design center in Fort Wayne, the French doors to my office are permanently open. I actually have to move a chair to shut them. My executive assistant, Debbie, sits at her own desk right outside my office doors, and given that they're always open, we can carry on a conversation without either of us getting up from our separate desk chairs. Except that I'm hardly ever sitting down. My friend and colleague Joan Maxwell used to say, "If I need to find you, I never look in your office."

It's true that I'm hardly ever there because I've found that by getting up from behind my desk and walking around the building I learn the most about the people with whom I work and the projects they're working on. I have had some of my best conversations at the coffee machine and in the ladies' restroom. As I explained to our financial advisor, George Cook, when he reprimanded Pat and me for making too many expensive phone calls in the early days—you make the best connections when you actually *talk* to people.

At Vera Bradley

we believe in creating an atmosphere

where people can connect. 1997.

This was the dilemma I presented to Vera Bradley's board of directors a few years ago. At that time, we were in five buildings located in the Fort Wayne area, which meant that many of the employees never had an opportunity to interact with, and sometimes even meet with, each other.

AN OPEN DOOR SAYS: *I WANT TO BE INVOLVED.*

"We all should be under one roof," I said. The board was skeptical due to the high cost of breaking leases and new construction. Well, this is one of those instances where I jokingly pulled the "Barb card" and suggested they reconsider. (I actually have standard-size business cards in my wallet that say "Barb" on the front and "Because I said so" on the back.) I played it here because I believe so much in creating an atmosphere where people can connect. "Our departments are not isolated," I explained. "We are interconnected and we should all work *together.*" Plus, some of our most inspired ideas for moving the company forward have been born when people with different perspectives talked with each other.

After designing a practical building plan, the board agreed. In fact, the vote was unanimous and now the Vera Bradley corporate office has a single address.

HAVE AN *Open Door* POLICY

When you open doors, people inevitably walk in. And when you move through the world with an "openness" about you, you make connections wherever you go.

KEEP IT REAL

Pat and I were exhibiting at the Javits Center gift show in New York in 1989 when a woman dressed head to toe in black walked into our very colorful booth. It was obvious to me that she was a true New Yorker. The woman introduced herself as Kay LeRoy and said she was with New York's Tavern on the Green in Central Park. "I'm interested in buying for the restaurant's gift shop," she said as she handed us her card and requested we set up a meeting.

How thrilling, we thought. *The buyer for the very famous Tavern on the Green wants our designs!* Of course we'd meet with her.

A few days later, we were invited to lunch at the restaurant. Kay led us back through the main dining room to a private table beautifully set for three. As we made introductory small talk, Kay apologized as we continued to be interrupted by staff members who came into the room to ask her questions. Finally I said to Kay, "So what exactly do you do here?" I assumed she was a buyer, but her influence appeared to extend far beyond the gift shop.

"I own it."

"You own Tavern on the Green," I blurted out. "You mean, you own the *whole place*?"

"I do," she said, amused by my stunned reaction, "and I'd love Vera Bradley to develop a pattern exclusively for the gift store. Would that interest you?"

"Absolutely," Pat and I practically said in unison.

The pattern we created was called, appropriately, "Tavern on the Green" and had a design that was reminiscent of Central Park, including birds, flowers, and a dense landscape of trees. The pattern was a huge success and as we continued to design for the restaurant, our business partnership grew into a friendship. Whenever we traveled to New York, Kay would invite Pat and me to her wonderful parties. She was a local celebrity in her own right, and Kay was also married to Warner LeRoy who founded LeRoy Adventures, which owned and operated the flamboyant Maxwell's Plum, the elegant Russian Tea Room, York Cinema, and Six Flags Great Adventure and Safari amusement park. To say that this couple was well connected was an understatement.

Kay and Warner seemed to know everyone. And they loved to throw parties at their apartment in The Dakota. The first time Pat and I were invited over to the famous residential building on the Upper West Side known for its prestige and exclusivity, we could hardly believe it. *How did two girls from Fort Wayne, Indiana, end up here?* We'd heard the stories that not just anyone gets into The Dakota and we loved that she'd invited us into her celebrity mix. I will never forget the party that Pat, Kim Colby, Peer, and I attended. At one point during the evening, I watched Peer talking with the very reconizable Yoko Ono. As she smiled up at him, I imagined that he was charming her as he did so many people. When he joined up with me later, he recounted their conversation.

"She asked me who I was with and I pointed over to you. 'My wife—the redhead.' And then I asked her—'Is your husband here?'"

Yoko had loved this, Kay later told me, because it was so rare for her to feel a sense of anonymity. Peer hadn't realized she was John Lennon's widow. He had no idea who she was! He'd taken an interest in her for no other reason than he was interested in whomever he met. That was so Peer. He spoke to Yoko just as he would anyone else—not as a celebrity but as a real person. I think that's why Kay liked having Pat and me around, too. We never pretend to be anything more than real people.

BE THE *Real* THING

True talent rises to the top and doesn't need to be dressed up. Similarly, the people who are the most real and authentic stand out in a party. What would happen if you showed up at your next meeting, lunch date, or parent-teacher conference just as *you*?

In my experience, the people who get the most attention and respect are those who don't apologize for who they are, or pretend to be someone else.

CHOOSE CAREFULLY

When I'm invited to speak to college students about how best to choose an internship program or a first place of employment, I always say: *choose carefully.* Really consider the employer, the environment, and the people with whom you'll be spending many of your days. It's the new home you will be living in. Ask yourself: do their values match up with mine? This is an important consideration wherever you are or whatever your age and stage in your life.

In a sense, when you accept any job, take on a project or partnership, or put yourself in a new environment, you're aligning yourself with a certain set of standards, expectations, and practices—either of the company, your client, or the group of people you've surrounded yourself with. So choose people you respect and environments that reflect your personal standards and beliefs. This is how you maintain your integrity (and also steer clear of places that don't mirror you). A few things to keep in mind when you evaluate any situation that you're considering becoming a part of:

ALIGN YOURSELF WITH PEOPLE YOU RESPECT AND ENVIRONMENTS THAT REFLECT YOUR PERSONAL STANDARDS AND BELIEFS.

Observe the environment: what is the mood? Welcoming? Warm? Or is it an atmosphere of intimidation? Are doors open or shut?

Observe the reception: how were you greeted by the receptionist, the employees, and top management? Warmly and with interest? Did people look up from their desks and acknowledge you? Did people stop in the halls and speak with you? Or were people too much in a hurry, or distracted, to give you their energy or time?

Observe the interactions between people. How do employees interact with each other? Do they seem friendly or competitive? Are people lighthearted or looking stressed?

Finally, ask yourself: how do I feel in this environment? Be honest with your-self—does it feel like a good fit? Is it a match to *you*?

I once visited an exclusive spa in Miami Beach in the hopes of landing a sales account. It was an absolutely beautiful and inviting setting, and their attention to detail was a perfect match to the Vera Bradley brand. When I showed up with several duffel bags full of product samples, the doorman, assuming that I was checking in, graciously took them from me. But the minute I said I was meeting with the buyer of their gift store, all pretenses stopped. He literally dropped my bags in the middle of the reception hall and hastily walked me to the back of the house.

That was my first indication that something wasn't matching up. I was shown into a dark and messy back room that didn't reflect the overall look and feel of the spa. This told me immediately that the company didn't respect their employ-ees enough to make their space as warm and welcoming as the rest of the prop-erty. I soon learned that they didn't highly regard their guests, either. The gift shop buyer and the manager of the spa began gossiping in front of me about

Headquarters, Fort Wayne, Indiana.
We've come a long way from those early
days of cutting out patterns on a Ping-Pong table.

HAVE THE COURAGE TO SAY NO WHEN A SITUATION DOESN'T FEEL RIGHT.

their celebrity clientele—the alcoholic, the one struggling in her marriage, the one suffering from weight issues, and on and on. *Why were they telling me this?* I was shocked by their cattiness and indiscretion, and by their false act. They presented themselves so glamorously in the front, but it was a different story in the back.

In that moment, I knew that I didn't want to do business with them. Their values, standards, and practices were a mismatch with my own, and also, they weren't representative of Vera Bradley.

I knew in my heart that our product did not belong there and so even though it felt a bit awkward to close this account before we even opened it, I followed my mother's lead—have the courage to say no when a situation doesn't feel right.

I'll never forget the time I tried over and over to get a client to pay his outstanding balance. Finally the man replied via fax saying, "I don't owe you this money. And, even if I did, I doubt Vera Bradley would drop dead over this amount." Turns out, Mother had indeed died that week at age eighty-two. I faxed the obituary to the gentleman with a note that read, "You do and she did."

Every day, I hold our company up to the standards of Vera. I'm pretty unyielding that her name not be associated with practices and values that weren't hers. This came into play again when the company began a new fragrance line. We were searching for a partner that would help us with packaging and one company in particular recommended a design that added a "lift" to the bottom of the box. This would make the actual size of the perfume bottle appear bigger on the outside than on the inside, they explained. *But that's dishonest,* I thought, *and it's not how we do things. And Mother definitely wouldn't approve.*

WHAT DO YOU *Value?*

At Vera Bradley we don't hang our company values up on a wall. We hope that they come across in the way we communicate, conduct, and carry ourselves every day of the year.

What values are driving your work and home life? Do they match up with your *true* values. . . what's *really* important to you? Choose your environment carefully and if the look and feel doesn't match your personal style, it may be time to change the scenery.

Color

Your

Work

FIND YOUR INSPIRATION

People often ask me where I get my inspiration, where the creative spark for our designs comes from. I'm never quite sure what to tell them. I could say that creative people influence me. Kit Kemp, cofounder and design director of Firmdale Hotels, is a shining example of this. Her unique designs explode with color, pattern, and texture. I'm inspired every time I walk through the spaces she creates. (And yes, I've been known to follow housekeeping in the hopes of sneaking a peek at her different hotel rooms. They each have their own special flair and I want to see them all!)

I could also say more broadly that travel awakens and broadens my senses and also inspires the brand. The design team travels all over the world to study emerging trends in fashion, and in many cases, the place itself influences our line. Africa, for example, is reflected in many of our bold designs. The elegance of Paris is stitched into our

I AM INSPIRED BY EVERYTHING—BY THE ORDINARY AND THE EXTRAORDINARY.

The Chrysler bag,

inspired by the iconic building.

timeless pieces and my Florida roots will always run through our patterns in bright and sunny colors. Oh, and don't let me forget New York! I find inspiration on nearly every street corner in this city. Our exclusive collection of duffels for our SoHo store was designed with an empire state of mind; each piece inspired by a symbol of New York City. And though I've gone to the top of the Empire State Building, taken the Staten Island Ferry, and explored the Metropolitan Museum of Art, the truth is that I'd rather take off the museum headphones and be out on the street observing and absorbing life at my own pace. That's where the true color is.

Because the true answer to the question: where do I get my inspiration, is EVERYWHERE! I am inspired by everything—by the ordinary and the extraordinary and by creativity itself. There isn't one single source. I get my inspiration out in the world, and I impress upon my grandchildren to see as much of it as they can. I tell them: by experiencing and being *in* the world, you inevitably gain a more colorful perspective than you ever will by studying any one place.

Wherever I am, I like to get outside and walk. I notice details everywhere I go. It could be a door handle that catches my eye, a paint color, or a single bloom. I let my eye and my sense of curiosity take me in all directions. That's how I ended up in Madam Hadem's.

I was visiting my son Jimmy and his wife, Laura, at their home in Marblehead, Massachusetts, when I went out shopping alone one day. I walked into a quaint boutique and found a pair of pumps I liked. I asked the store clerk if she had them in a size nine. She looked at me puzzled. "No, ma'am, I only have the one pair. This is a secondhand store."

"Oh." I laughed, now understanding the name of the shop—Madam Had 'Em.

I have no bias toward where I shop (if the shoe fits, it doesn't matter if it's off a consignment rack or from Bergdorf Goodman), nor do I pick and choose where I find inspiration. Rather, I let inspiration find me.

I'm influenced by the world around me, and also by the people in my life. Not only do I make a point to surround myself with friends and colleagues of different

NOTICE THE DETAILS. THERE'S INSPIRATION TO BE FOUND EVERYWHERE, JUST BY BEING IN THE WORLD.

ages and interests, experiences and stories, but also the walls in my home and at the office are covered with photos of the people I love and admire, past and present. My dear friends Mary Sloane, Mary Ann, and Glenna; my children and grandchildren; my husband, Peer; and Mother and Dad surround me every day. My whole life, in a sense, is framed on the walls. Peer was the same way. His office was a collage of memories.

He defended his orderly mess by saying, "A clean stable is a sign of a dead horse." I remember noticing once after a new employee set up his office that he had only a single picture frame on his desk. It was so stark and impersonal. I asked him, "Why the one picture?" He looked back at me, baffled. "At my last job, we were allowed only one personal photo. Should I take this one down?"

"No," I encouraged him. "Please add *more.*"

WHAT *Delights* YOU?

Your workspace, or any space where you spend time, should be a reflection of what you love. When you surround yourself with the people and patterns that give you a lift, your life often becomes more inspired and creative. Look for ways to add a little more inspiration to your life today.

GO BIG

f you're inspired to make a change, create something new, or elevate what you already do, not only do I encourage you to go for it, I also encourage you to GO BIG. That was the attitude Pat and I took when we pitched ourselves to the Chicago gift show in 1983. At that time the Chicago gift show was one of the largest and most attended shows in the country, with hundreds of vendors displaying their new products. It was where all the big buyers came to place their orders for the next season, where anyone wanting to gain national attention and sell more broadly wanted to be.

Up until this point, Pat and I had been selling small to medium orders of Vera Bradley bags to local gift and specialty shops, as well as ladies' clothing stores in Fort Wayne and the surrounding cities. I kept duffels and totes with me at all times, so if I was traveling I'd stop in to the local gift store and—hopefully—make a sale. I was successful more often than not, and most of the stores that carried us were selling out of inventory and reordering more. They loved the color, the functionality, and the detail. "Your bags pop like a bouquet of flowers," they told us. Pat and I were confident that we'd created a beautiful solution for women just like us, and so we were challenged to think bigger. How could we get Vera Bradley bags into more hands?

The gift-show circuit. That was a world I knew. Dad was a sales rep for Victory Light Candles and, as a young girl, I'd attended many gift shows with him. I understood the power of getting noticed by independent gift retailers in an exhibit hall of this size and influence. The gift show could become our backbone of distribution. But at that time, over thirty years ago, handbags and luggage were not an included category in any national gift show. (Now, I'm happy to say, they're up and down every aisle.) But because I'm a firm believer in the saying, *whether you think you can or you think you can't, you're probably right,* I picked up the phone and called someone in management. *I'm going to assume they'll say yes,* I told myself.

I asked for a booth, explaining that handbags should be included in the show because they make perfect gifts. "We don't have a category for handbags," the man on the other end of the line said. The show was divided into product categories and booths were placed accordingly. "You should try and get a booth in the apparel show." But we didn't want a booth in apparel because that show was fashion-focused and that's not how we saw the Vera Bradley products we were creating. Not yet, anyway.

"Wouldn't you give a handbag to your wife or college-age daughter?" I asked. I wasn't going to give up that easily. While he didn't see a place for us, I did. I believed in what we were creating and in what we could become and I projected that bigger mind-set into the conversation.

"I have nowhere to put you," he said again. "I can't put you in china, imports, or men's gifts. Like I said, there's no category for handbags."

"Then create one."

He finally relented and agreed. In part, I think, just to shut me up. My tenacity was rewarded with a ten-by-ten-foot booth in the last aisle in the lower level of the McCormick Place convention center. You couldn't find us even with a map. I didn't care. We were in.

ALWAYS BELIEVE IN WHAT YOU CREATE.

Pat and I gave our space the same special touches as we give to our products. We laid out a rug on the floor, wallpapered the inside of our cabinets with brightly colored patterns, and hung our fabrics to create a backdrop. (Eventually, I would go even *bigger* by hanging a chandelier from the inside of our booth at every show.) We did all this to make the space inviting

and comfortable, like our own homes. And also memorable, like the home you're always happy to return to. I understood that every detail counts. Together, they create an experience and that first booth at the Chicago gift show received the same level of attention to detail we give to our Vera Bradley showroom on Fifth Avenue today.

Pat and I are positive people, but nobody was more surprised than we were when the show opened and, despite our remote location, our booth was jammed!

For five days, we worked the booth, and I mean—we really *worked it*. From eight in the morning until six in the evening, we welcomed everyone who walked by. "You never meet a stranger," Dad used to say and I followed his example. We treated every single person like a friend. Pat and I became better at "selling" simply by having real conversations with people, and we'd rush back to the hotel at the end of the day to add up our totals. I'd call Dad, excited to share with him who wrote the biggest order and he'd say, "That's great, and it'll be even more exciting when you have the reorders." With this comment, he was encouraging us to continue to build upon every relationship.

After that first successful year at McCormick Place we were back the next. I could hardly wait to get there. This time, we brought along Mother, my sister Joan, and my friend Glenna, who were some of the company's first sales reps. With more than twice as many hands on deck, working the show really didn't feel like work at all. Essentially, our booth became the biggest party at McCormick Place. Our positive energy, friendliness, and attitude of keeping the *f* in fun brought people in. Our booth seemed always to be busy and full of people. I

> ## WHEN YOU BELIEVE IN WHAT YOU DO AND HAVE FUN DOING IT, YOU ATTRACT THE ATTENTION OF PEOPLE AROUND YOU.

remember when a woman from a much larger and established gift company came into our booth and pulled me aside. "I've been watching you girls. There is so much energy in your booth. I wonder, would you be interested in repping *my* company?"

You see, when you believe in what you do and have fun doing it, you attract the attention of people around you. They want in on whatever you're selling. Our booth at the Chicago gift show won "Best Overall" for multiple years in a row. I believe this is because we continued to create an environment that made everyone who entered it feel good.

It was the third year of us setting up our booth in the lower level of McCormick Place and the vendor next door was a company that sold a variety of magnet items. One afternoon I took five minutes to wander over and buy a pair of faux diamond, magnet stud earrings. I dropped them in my purse and then forgot about them. After the show that evening, I went to a rooftop party for the exhibitors. There were probably a thousand people in attendance, but my eye was drawn to a little girl standing off by herself in a Pierre Deux dress (a complementary brand I admired). I walked over to her and said hello. I remembered the magnet earrings and pulled them out of my purse. "Would you like these? They'd look cute on you." She took them from me with a smile and went skipping off. A few minutes later she returned holding the hand of her mother, and wearing the diamond studs.

"My name is Ye and this is my daughter, Thea. Who are you sitting with tonight?" She was referring to the program directly following the party.

"I'm here alone," I said.

"Then why don't you join us at our table?"

I accepted her invitation and an hour or so later as the program was about to start, I overheard Ye whisper to her daughter, "Daddy is going to speak now." As soon as she said it, Will Little stepped onto the stage. I was floored. *Her father is Will Little? Of George Little Management that owns the Chicago gift show and EVERY MAJOR GIFT SHOW ACROSS THE COUNTRY!? What are the odds?*

After the show, Will Little joined our table. "This is Barbara Bradley," Ye said to her husband. I smiled and shook his hand. "She has a company named Vera Bradley that makes women's handbags," Ye continued. "They're a relatively new exhibitor."

While I was thrilled to be introduced to the head of the gift show, I was even more elated when the next day Will Little appeared at our booth! After a few minutes of taking a studied look around, he said, "Well, we've got to get you upstairs."

And just like that, we moved uptown.

The next year, our booth was in the first row on the first floor of McCormick Place. We had the privilege of sharing the exhibition hall with Jelly Belly, Burt's Bees, and Thymes Candles. Oh, the company we kept! This front-row position gave us maximum exposure and before we knew it, we'd gone from small to big.

What started as a friendly encounter with a little girl led to a serendipitous connection that, in many ways, set the course forward for Vera Bradley and changed the direction of my life. The experience was yet another powerful reminder of the importance of making friends wherever you go and believing in yourself and whatever it is you're creating. This magical combination will draw the right people to you like a magnet.

THINK BIG. *Go Big.*

Whatever your work, how you spend your time, or what you create, believe in it. And don't be afraid to think and go big. Sure, it can be hard to have that belief in yourself and to find the courage to think big in the beginning, but that's when you really need it most. Confidence inspires people. Start thinking bigger today.

THERE'S ENOUGH FOR EVERYONE

We were the first company to display handbags and luggage at the Chicago gift show but that quickly changed. Before long, there were handbag companies up and down the aisles of every major gift show, from New York to Atlanta to San Francisco. In 2000, I wandered into the showroom of another handbag company and was curtly asked to leave. "Why?" I responded. Because I was the "competition." *How unfortunate*, I thought, *we have so much in common.* Shouldn't we automatically like each other for being in the same industry and having a similar passion?

There are many brands out there similar to Vera Bradley and we're all doing well in our own way. Of course, we don't like to see an obvious knockoff and we also try to avoid looking too much like another brand by maintaining our unique identity. But in general, I consider it a high compliment when another company creates something similar to ours. It's a big world out there. There's enough room for everyone. We can all do what we do and there's enough success to go around.

I once sat down to dinner with the senior buyers for two competing American upscale department stores: Dillard's and Von Maur. Both stores carried Vera

IF YOU BELIEVE IN WHAT YOU DO AND DO IT TO THE BEST OF YOUR ABILITY, WHY WORRY ABOUT WHAT EVERYONE ELSE IS DOING?

Bradley and I knew both sets of the female buyers well. They had never met each other, however, and judging by how outwardly competitive the two stores were, I imagined their buyers would not choose to have dinner together. I was determined, though, to bring them to the same table because I felt certain this group of women would all get along. Again, why wouldn't they? We all work in the same industry. We have so much in common! So I invited both sets of buyers to join me at my home in Fort Wayne for dinner. Well, what do you think happened when they all arrived? They enjoyed each other fully. Where these women would probably have never met on their own, the group of us sat comfortably around my dinner table until nearly midnight, swapping stories about business and our personal lives. By the end of the night, we were laughing together like only friends do.

(My insider tip: call a meeting of the minds at a round table. Whether it's in my own home or at the office, I prefer to meet, sit, and dine with people at a round table. Not only does this circular design allow for every person to easily speak and be heard by all, but also it positions the group equally. No one is at the head. No one person, or voice, is more important. And this fosters inclusion, rather than competition.)

If you believe in what you do and do it to your best ability, why worry about what everyone else is doing? Just stay true to yourself. I respect and am inspired by what others can do well and I'm happy when they're successful. Coach, for example, is considered a competing brand to ours, but I don't see it that way. It's not us against them. Rather, they are a *complementary* brand. We each do what we do well, and while we have products that are similar, we each have our own look and style. There's enough room for both of us. And thank goodness, diversity of preferences makes the world more colorful.

THERE'S ROOM FOR *Everyone*

Not too long ago, I ran into a woman from another "competing" brand at the AmericasMart in Atlanta. I walked right up to her and said, "I love your new line," and she responded with, "And I'm so inspired by what *you're* doing." There's enough room for everyone, so keep creating and doing what you do. If you believe in yourself and stay true to you, you'll succeed.

ACT AS IF

Sometimes in order to go big, you have to *act as if*—meaning, you have to act as if you're big before you really are. This is akin to "dressing the part." In the beginning, we did a lot of "acting as if." When the phone rang, we'd answer it and say, "Vera Bradley . . . hold on, let me transfer you . . ." even if there was no one to transfer the call to!

In the first several years of exhibiting at gift shows, we'd drive up to Chicago from Fort Wayne and stay at the Whitehall Hotel. This historic downtown hotel was well above our price range at the time, but the guests of the Whitehall represented the customers we wanted to buy Vera Bradley. I strongly believe in surrounding yourself with the type of people you want in both your professional and personal life. That's really the best way to redesign your life to match what you want next. So Pat and I, along with Mother, my sister Joan, and my dear friend Mary Sloane would check into the hotel and share rooms. This is how we could afford for all of us to stay there. Besides, "bunking" together was fun. It was like going back to camp or living in a sorority house. Also, we'd ask for a room on the concierge floor because we knew that's where many of the big buyers attending the Chicago gift show also stayed and this would potentially provide

I STRONGLY BELIEVE IN SURROUNDING YOURSELF WITH THE TYPE OF PEOPLE YOU WANT IN BOTH YOUR PROFESSIONAL AND PERSONAL LIFE. THAT'S REALLY THE BEST WAY TO REDESIGN YOUR LIFE TO MATCH WHAT YOU WANT NEXT.

us with even more opportunities to make connections after the show.

Overnight parking at the Whitehall was no more affordable for us then than the rooms but on the second day of the show, we received a lucky break. Dwight, the doorman, with whom I became friendly, had heard us complaining back and forth about the garage fees and offered us a helpful solution. He said, "I could drive your car home at night and bring it back in the morning. Then it won't cost you a thing." Dwight explained that he regularly took the train to work, but if he were to drive our car in during the day, he could park it on his street at night. While many people I've told this story to say they'd be too nervous to hand the keys to their car over to someone they hardly knew, Dwight had been accommodating to us from the start. That was enough for me. Sure, I didn't know much more about him than that he worked at the Whitehall, nor was I familiar with the suburb of Chicago where he lived, but my instincts told me to trust him. I said, "Sure, why not? This is perfect. It solves both of our problems. You get a car to drive and we don't have to pay to park it."

When he pulled up to the Whitehall in our station wagon the next morning, I knew I was right—people generally like to help other people. Dwight had just saved us a significant amount in overnight parking fees and we'd saved him his train fare. We did this car exchange for the remaining three days of the show— and for *years* after that. We'd pull up our car at the end of the day, hand the keys over to Dwight, and he would drive it home. We started referring to the Whitehall as the "Dwighthall."

ACT AS IF!

In your pursuit to "act as if," you might have to use your imagination. Sometimes, you have to do the unexpected. And sometimes you have to ask for help. Don't hesitate. Most people enjoy helping others. Besides, it won't be long before people will be asking for *your* help!

SOMETIMES WRONG, NEVER IN DOUBT

The day we moved the company out of my basement and into our first real office was exciting. We no longer had to cut our tote and duffel bag patterns on the family Ping-Pong table! Still, our new home was far from luxurious: we all sat in a single room at card tables converted into makeshift desks. And by all of us, I mean the *six of us*. In the windowless, upstairs board room of Taylor-Martin (my then-husband's paper company), we worked side by side with the use of one phone, one typewriter, and one three-drawer filing cabinet.

In those early days, we all pitched in wherever needed. If there wasn't much going on in the office, we'd help out in shipping, rolling up our sleeves and stacking products on our single pallet for the forklift operator. And we all took turns cutting patterns until we eventually bought an industry cutter and hired someone specifically for that job. (Good thing, too, because I once cut my toe horribly on it and had to use Vera Bradley fabric to wrap it. It continued to bleed so Pat drove me to the downtown ER and the nurse on duty said it was the best-looking tourniquet she'd ever seen.)

The early days were primitive. Not at all glamorous. But it was exciting and fun because Pat and I had surrounded ourselves with people who also believed in what we were creating. We had our small office staff and then we had our sales team. Our first salespeople—Vera, my sister Joan, friends Glenna, Mary Ann, and Mary Sloane—agreed to get paid when the company did. Not everyone would or could accept those terms, but friends and family will often take a chance on you when others won't, which is exactly why they were our first recruits.

As long as I've been in business, I've heard warnings against hiring "people you know." I've never understood this. Again, I want to work with people I like, with people I want to share a meal with and so for me, starting a company with some of my best friends and family members seemed like the most obvious choice. Even my then-thirteen-year-old-son Jimmy Byrne was thrown into the mix; we put him to work ironing trim in the afternoons after school.

Thirty years later, I can confidently say that we hired right because not only would I happily have dinner with any of the twenty-eight hundred employees at the company today, but many of the women we brought in at the start are still with us, including women like Elit Hoover, who was initially hired to be a monogrammer. Today, Elit is a key member of our design team, and draws nearly every flat sketch, complete with the measurements and specifications that become our proprietary Vera Bradley patterns. The "Elit" bag is named after her, and we've been naming bags after friends and employees since day one.

TRIAL AND ERROR IS THE ONLY WAY TO LEARN.

When I asked Mother if she wanted to be a rep in Miami, she jumped right on board as I imagined she would. (Just like Dad, Vera was a natural saleswoman. Her elegance disarmed you; she could practically sell you a bag just with her smile.) When I interviewed my

More than just the company's namesake,

Vera was a valuable member of our team.

Here she is with Pat.

friend Mary Ann for the job, we were sitting on the dock at Lake Gage in our bathing suits. She was teaching kindergarten part time and said, "Absolutely! Who wouldn't love to go into shops every day and meet other women?" When I asked my college friend Glenna, who was still at home with her children, if she wanted to help, she became our rep in Birmingham, Michigan, nearly overnight. I hired my friend Joan Maxwell at a bar in Atlanta called Pittypat's Porch, and I hired my niece Kathy when she was just twenty-four and right out of college. She's stayed with the company ever since and is one of our top sales reps today.

None of us was trained to sell but we learned quickly, mostly by trial and error and by following one of our early company mantras: *sometimes wrong, never in doubt.* Accept that mistakes may happen. (After all, this is part of the creative process.) But don't doubt your natural ability to create and fulfill your vision.

TRIAL & ERROR IS THE WAY TO GO

If you truly want to forge your own path, you're going to have to be open to making mistakes. Just keep to your course and surround yourself with people who also believe in what you are creating.

CULTIVATE A SISTERHOOD

The bond that was formed between all of us in the beginning has evolved into the sisterhood culture that defines Vera Bradley. More than just a nice way to do business, that culture is also responsible for spurring the company's growth. As the orders for our bags grew, so did the bonds between women all over the country. As we traveled from town to town visiting colleges and stores, we started to notice how strong this sisterhood of the traveling quilt had become. It was as if by carrying a Vera Bradley bag you were instantly initiated into a kindred sorority. My daughters Amy and Joanie, who were both in the Kappa Kappa Gamma house at Michigan State in the early days of the company, described how the girls carrying Vera Bradley totes and duffels exchanged an unspoken "wink," as if to say, "we're of a similar quilt." I'm proud to say that this

CULTIVATE A CULTURE OF NICE WHEREVER YOU GO.

shared connection often leads to lasting friendships. And it happens all over—not just on college campuses.

The first time I saw a woman walking down the street on Martha's Vineyard carrying one of our bags, I impulsively went up to her and introduced myself. She threw her arms around me and hugged me tightly. Everywhere we went, we started to hear stories that told us that we'd created more than a bag. There was the woman who lived alone and after her beloved cocker spaniel passed away, she tearfully drove to her local Vera Bradley store because she said, "I knew the staff would be sympathetic." Then there was the woman who got stuck in the Chicago airport. Her connecting flight was canceled and the next available plane wouldn't depart until the following morning. She frantically looked around the airport for another woman with a Vera Bradley bag to share a hotel room with because, she said, "I knew she'd be nice." Without really trying to, we'd created a culture of nice, where our customers were more than our friends. They were our *sisters*.

Where you won't see women on Fifth Avenue stopping to introduce themselves because they happen to be carrying the same style of Louis Vuitton bag, it's not at all uncommon for women carrying Vera Bradley to embrace one another and exchange e-mail addresses in an airport security line. I've received many letters over the years that describe how our customers consider themselves part of the Vera Bradley "family." One of my favorites is the story of a young man bringing his girlfriend home to meet his family for the first time. When she walked through the door with a Vera Bradley duffel, his four older sisters nodded to each other in agreement. "She's okay," they said. "She's one of us."

STRONGER TOGETHER

When you know who your audience is and what your values are, you can start to build a sisterhood. And when you build a sisterhood, anything can happen.

Who is in your sorority?

THE CULTURE OF COLOR

In the early days when Pat and I were exhibiting at the Chicago gift show, we never could figure out what to wear in the booth. There was so much color in the space already. What could we wear, I wondered, that would blend with the current designs? And so I had the idea: what if we fashioned outfits created from Vera Bradley fabrics? A week before the gift show, a friend and I were up at my cottage on Lake Gage. We drew up a few simple patterns, pulled out my Singer sewing machine, and went to work. The result was a one-size-fits-all skirt with an elastic waist and a border trim sash, a camisole, and a matching double-breasted blouse with puff sleeves and eyelets on the collar.

We proudly wore our matching Vera Bradley outfits the next week at the gift show. I look back at pictures and wonder, *Honestly, what* were *we thinking*? We really did look like bridesmaids—or perhaps even sister wives. But everyone loved the custom clothes, and wanted them for themselves. While we had no intention of selling the cotton

> PASSION AND PAISLEY ARE CONTAGIOUS.

off our backs, we started writing orders anyhow. Pat, who didn't attend this particular show, called at the end of the day and asked what was selling best. "The outfits," I said.

"What outfits?"

And that was the year we got into the apparel business.

In 2005 we made another natural transition into home goods. People had been approaching us since some of our very first gift shows to buy the rugs, throw pillows, and chairs we used to decorate our booth. But since most of the pieces were from my own home, we didn't sell them. But with every passing year, we had to fight off buyers who wanted to purchase my living room set. I finally concluded that since interior design is my second love, and the Vera Bradley fabrics and prints seemed to lend themselves so well to furniture, why not give them what they want? This was another one of those moments when I realized—if you build it, and *believe in it*, they will come. Passion and paisley are contagious.

Today, one of the most remarkable examples of our "if you build it" business philosophies can be witnessed at the annual Vera Bradley outlet sale. This began as a small tent sale in 1985 and has evolved into a coliseum sale where last year sixty-five thousand women from ages eight to eighty from all fifty states visited Fort Wayne for this Coachella-type event to purchase thousands of items. While I know that the sale draws people because of the discounts—and I've even seen women dive headfirst into the clearance bins—I also know they come for the feeling of sisterhood and shared history, especially those who have been carrying our bags and backpacks since childhood and throughout college and into adulthood (I recently met a woman who has sixty-five Vera Bradley bags in her collection dating back to our very first designs). Upon hearing this, I gave *her* a hug.

This family affair, which often includes members of my own family working the registers, has become a yearly pilgrimage for many sisters, mothers, daughters, and best friends, and many treat the weekend as a girlfriends' getaway. I like to think that the thousands of women who come back year after year wearing their VB OR BUST! T-shirts and carrying their inherited or very first monogrammed bags do so because they believe in the culture we've created, one built on the strength, support, and love of family and friends.

Material girls. At one of the early gift shows wearing our matching Vera Bradley outfits. (Mimi, Glenna, Barbara, and Mary Ann.)

THE COMPANY YOU KEEP

Surrounding yourself with talent is important, but in my opinion the strongest teams come willingly and are excited to be a part of what you're building, creating, and doing. Invite the right people to jump on board and be part of your dream. Often, when you build on your dream, the culture will call the right people—without even being asked.

ADD A BIG CAUSE TO YOUR PURPOSE

Whether you're building a family, a business, or designing the perfect handbag, supporting a cause that reflects your values—something greater than yourself and your work—will enrich the work you do. In 1992, six years after the company was formed, my college roommate, best friend, and a rep for Vera Bradley, Mary Sloane, died of breast cancer at age fifty. The same disease had taken Mary's mother and grandmother. My friend was fun, beautiful, and full of life. We clicked from the moment we first met and were thereafter practically inseparable. Throughout the years we attended college together at Marymount, I'd bring her home during spring break and holidays to Miami Beach because her father was a four-star general stationed in Okinawa, Japan. Flying to Florida only required a simple weekender bag.

Vera and Ed more or less adopted Mary and she became like a sister to me. Every time we saw each other it was like a day hadn't passed and by the time she was diagnosed, we'd seen each other through it all—graduation, weddings,

My dear friend Mary Sloane.

She was like a sister to me.

the birth of our children, and many years working together for Vera Bradley. Her death shook
me profoundly, and I began to notice that so many
of the women I knew had suffered similar losses.
Breast cancer was looming for countless women,
and so after losing our dear friend, Pat and I said,
"Enough is enough. We have to do something."

We felt that it was time to take action and share
what we could, which was our time, resources,
relationships, and a strong belief in the importance of giving back. We pulled all of this out of
our bags and went to work.

> SUPPORTING A CAUSE THAT REFLECTS YOUR VALUES—SOMETHING GREATER THAN YOURSELF AND YOUR WORK—WILL ENRICH THE WORK YOU DO.

In 1994 Pat and I created a women's charitable golf tournament to raise
money for breast cancer research. The first year we set out to raise twenty thousand dollars. Mind you, we didn't know the first thing about running a golf tournament; we'd never done anything like it. We both played golf and we knew how
to throw a good party, but that was about as far as our expertise went. This didn't
stop us. We had a goal in mind and we approached the challenge the same way
as we did when starting the company—ready, fire, aim. Don't overthink it; make
a commitment and then figure out how to do it. And also, make it fun!

That first year we raised sixty-four thousand dollars, more than triple our
goal. I can't tell you how rewarding it was to give those proceeds to the American
Cancer Society, knowing that they would fund breast cancer research, educa-
tion, and patient services. Four years later, we created the Vera Bradley Foundation for Breast Cancer and offered all proceeds to the Indiana University School
of Medicine. The president of the university asked us if we would pledge $1.2
million over the next five years, a sum that would allow us to endow a chair in
oncology for breast cancer research.

How will we raise that much money? we wondered. Then we quickly accepted
the challenge. We thought, *If we don't raise it, what are they going to do—throw*

us in jail? Well, they didn't throw us in jail. We raised the $1.2 million in less than five years, and since then the event has become the nation's largest amateur women's golf and tennis charity tournament and Indiana's premiere women's sporting event. The Vera Bradley Classic has grown from one eighteen-hole golf competition to an additional nine-hole tourney and a multidivision tennis tournament where professional sports legends and celebrities have played along with friends and families. The Classic, along with other signature events for the Vera Bradley Foundation for Breast Cancer, has raised over $28 million to date to support critical advancements in breast cancer research. For every dollar donated to the foundation, eighty-seven cents goes directly toward research at the Indiana University Melvin and Bren Simon Cancer Center in Indianapolis, Indiana.

Pat and I started our foundation many years before most companies routinely supported a cause. We were one of the first to marshal company resources of all kinds as a means for supporting something that we felt strongly about. We didn't do it because it was on-trend or to leverage as a marketing tool, but because we believed heading off this disease is important to do to give more mothers the chance to become grandmothers, more girls the chance to become women, and more women the chance to become whomever and whatever they wish. I don't know many women who haven't been touched, in some way, by the disease and it was so personal to us because of Mary.

Today, the foundation's mission is woven into the very fabric of Vera Bradley and is part of the company culture. I can hardly separate the two; it's just who we are and it's made us a stronger community. Our employees, business partners, customers, and the friends who share our purpose seem to be as dedicated to finding an end to breast cancer as we are. Just drive through Fort Wayne during the month of May and there's hardly a street that isn't decorated with beautiful pink ribbons to show the local support in the fight against breast cancer. In 2016, local businesses and individuals joined together to "turn the town pink" by raising over $74,000. And speaking of pink, there doesn't seem to be a single woman who works in the Fort Wayne office who doesn't own her version of a little pink dress. At the Vera Bradley design center, pink never falls out of trend.

When my grandchildren were a bit younger they, too, got involved in the cause in their own way. One year, Henry sold pink jerseys to his lacrosse team, Gavin and Bradley made and sold pink bracelets at their schools, and for many years, my grandchildren set up a pink lemonade stand on the golf course of the tournament. At the end of the event, they'd present their own check to the foundation. A perfect example of when life throws you lemons, make lemonade.

I remember one time when the event fell on one of the rainiest days of the year. The head of event and culinary services called me from the golf course. "Barbara," he said. "I don't want you to be disappointed so I want to prepare you for a low turnout. In my experience, when it rains like this people do not come out to a tented event." Well, do you know what? They did. The rain and wind went sideways that day, and still there was not a single no-show and I think that's because our attendees have adopted our passion for the cause. No matter the weather, there was no way they were missing it.

To extend to my own family the value of giving back that is so intrinsic to the Vera Bradley culture, I created a birthday tradition with my grandchildren. There are twelve of them so birthdays come around quite frequently. Instead of trying to stay on top of each of their individual and evolving tastes, I give them money. Now, this is not a cop-out by their overly scheduled grandmother. The money I give them serves as part gift to them and with a caveat that is meant to inspire generosity and involvement in something bigger than them. I say, "You get to spend some of this money on you and then you must give the rest away." It doesn't matter to whom or where. It could be to someone who needs

GIVING OF YOURSELF LEADS YOU ON THE PATH TOWARD TRUE FULFILLMENT.

help or toward a cause that grabs their heart or they believe in. To my delight, all of my grandchildren have embraced this tradition. In fact, they are typically most excited to tell me what they did with the portion they gave away. I love hearing their stories and it's so touching to me to see how the tradition has made an impact. My grandson Christopher began giving small donations to the Special Olympics when he was a young boy. Throughout high school, he volunteered at the event itself. I'm proud that my way of gift-giving has led them to the ultimate gift of experiencing what it feels like to get behind a bigger cause in a real way.

BELIEVE

I believe, as Herman Melville said, "Our lives are connected by a thousand invisible threads, and along these sympathetic fibers, our actions run as causes and return to us as results."

What cause do you believe in? What speaks to your heart? How can you share your time, energy, or resources with the bigger causes that you are moved by?

You can always give something.

GIVE JUST FOR FUN

Since I'm in the gift business, I always have a gift on hand. When I travel, especially, I'll pack small gifts in my suitcase—for those I'm going to visit, and for others I might meet along the way. In fact, my gift giving starts at the airport. If I see someone carrying a Vera Bradley bag, I might stop her and give her a key chain or a cosmetic bag. When I stay in hotels, I leave a gift behind for housekeeping. When I get my hair cut, it's always fun to give my hairdresser a surprise. The last time I called the cable guy, I handed him a token of my appreciation. "A little something to give your girlfriend, wife, or daughter," I said. And when a friend is in the hospital, I love to send a small box of Vera Bradley gifts to hand out to those who are taking care of him or her.

I do this for no other reason than that it makes us both feel good, and these little gestures tend to be felt for years.

I was once entering a restaurant at Chicago's O'Hare Airport when the hostess commented on the scarf I was wearing.

"That's clever," she said. "How did you tie that? I can never figure out how to wear my scarves."

"I'll show you," I offered, and then after my demonstration I handed it to her and said, "Now you try."

She looped it through just as I had. "That's it," I said. "Now it's yours to keep."

When I can surprise and delight someone at the same time, this is also a gift for *me*. Giving, really, is its own reward. Once when I was traveling in Paris with Veronique, our vice president of product development, we wandered into a boutique. The saleswoman commented on Veronique's Vera Bradley quilted bag right away. In her French accent, she said, "I looooove it. Where can I get one?"

At that point, we didn't yet have an international Web site to order our products online so I turned to Veronique and said, "Why don't you just give it to her?"

"Huh?" Veronique answered, a little confused. "Then what will I carry all my stuff in?"

I looked around. "In a shopping bag," I said as I began to unload all the contents of Veronique's purse onto the saleswoman's countertop. This type of gesture I learned from my parents: if you have something that someone else doesn't have, then it's meant to be shared.

"This is for you," Veronique said somewhat reluctantly as she handed it to her.

"Oh, *merci*." The woman began to cry.

THE SMALLEST GIFT CAN MAKE SUCH A SIGNIFICANT IMPACT ON THE PERSON RECEIVING IT. AND SOMETIMES AN EVEN BIGGER IMPACT ON THE PERSON GIVING IT.

To this day, Veronique teases me for giving her bag away, but we got her another just like it and we made a woman in Paris feel very special.

Just as I encourage my grandchildren to pay a portion of their birthday money forward, I similarly encourage Vera Bradley employees to always be on the lookout for ways to make someone's day. My niece and Vera Bradley sales rep Kathy has a practice of handing out two gifts at a time: one to keep and one to share. She recounts the time she gave two

The Vera Bradley Foundation

is working for a future free from breast cancer.

Here I am with Pat and Dr. Bryan Schneider, MD, Indiana

University, proudly showcasing our fund-raising efforts.

small totes to the hotel receptionist where she was staying—one for you and one for a friend, she told her.

"After that," Kathy said, "she treated me like a celebrity. But I hadn't done it to win her over or get special treatment. I just wanted to spread our culture of nice."

It's always so amazing to me to see how the smallest gift can make such a significant impact on the person receiving it. On a whim one night when Peer and I were living in Chicago, he suggested we bring our doorman Melvin a candy bar. "He stands there all night," Peer said. "He's probably hungry and could use a treat." So, we bought Melvin a Milky Way bar at the corner store and brought it to him. Well, he acted like we'd just given him the keys to our apartment. He was so appreciative. So much so that the next time we were out we bought him another one. This became our routine, to the point where we didn't dare forget Melvin's Milky Way.

In another instance and while living in a different apartment in New York, I wondered what I could give my landlord that might make her smile. I'd never quite connected with her. I'd tried but no matter what I did or said, she was curt and dismissive. Add to that, she acted like we'd never met although I'd lived in the building for eight years! One day, I asked her point-blank, "Why are you so mean to me?"

She took offense. "I am *not* mean to you."

I said, "I'm from the Midwest and maybe we have a different way, but it's sad to me that you aren't friendlier."

She shrugged her shoulders and gave me a look like, *too bad.* She turned on her heels and walked away.

I was so frustrated with her, but still I decided to take the high road. After all, as they say, it's less crowded up there. Back in my apartment, I pulled out a beautiful blue Vera Bradley "Miller" bag that

I DECIDED TO TAKE THE HIGH ROAD. AFTER ALL, AS THEY SAY, IT'S LESS CROWDED UP THERE.

I'd never used. I wrapped it in tissue paper with a ribbon and wrote her a note: *Let's forget the past and start over today.*

When I gave it to her a day or so later, she looked up at me and gave way to emotion I hadn't seen before. "No one has ever given me anything," she said, clearly touched.

Probably because you aren't nice to anyone, I thought.

"How did you know blue was my favorite color?"

I didn't. I had just felt inspired to give it to her. Maybe because she seemed kind of blue and needed some cheering up.

Soon after that I moved from the building. I don't know if my thoughtfulness changed her. I do know that it shifted her in the moment, which is as much as I'd hoped my gift would do.

LITTLE THINGS *Mean* A LOT

In what way could you give a little more today? Who in your life might appreciate receiving something special? Or who in your life do you feel disconnected from and where a little act of kindness might bring you closer? A gift doesn't have to be a material object. The best gifts are often our smiles, our patience, and our attention. Challenge yourself to get into a regular habit of giving, and you'll likely begin to see how much more you receive in return.

Color Your Every Day

BE FUSSY

I believe in making a home wherever I go. That is, I like to create an environment where I feel at home and where anyone who enters feels welcome and at ease. Whether it's repositioning a vase of flowers to better catch the sunlight, turning on a corner lamp to add warmth to the room, or throwing a soft pillow onto the back of a chair for extra cushion, there are many ways—big and small—to shift the look and feel of any environment to be more inviting and cozy.

The *StrengthsFinder 2.0* assessment may not include a category that specifically identifies my attention to detail and urge to make a home wherever I go, but the "Developer" comes pretty close. The "Developer" regards every individual as a work in progress, as alive with possibilities. That's exactly how I feel about every room, and nearly every space I walk into.

I've had an eye for artistic possibilities for as long as I can remember. As a young girl, I'd go along with Mother to visit her friends' homes and would often spend the time studying the patterns on the wallpaper and the colors and textures of the throw rugs and drapes. My eyes have always been wide open; I notice it all. Over my lifetime my natural ability to "know it when I see it" has become a passion, not to

EVERY SPACE IS A WORK IN PROGRESS, ALIVE WITH POSSIBILITIES.

mention a cornerstone of Vera Bradley. (Some might call it an obsession.) I jokingly call this "Vera's curse," because Mother was the same way. Just as she did, I can walk into a room and know exactly what the space needs to be more beautiful. I recognize that not everyone sees what I do, even though it's something of a reflex for me. My grandchildren will tease me— "there goes Birdie being Birdie"— as they watch me inch the sofa over to the left and then back to the right to better align with the picture-perfect view out the window. I'm also guilty of walking through hotel lobbies straightening crooked lampshades.

My daughter Amy laughs at the times when she and her siblings were little and I'd stay up late at night, rearranging and redecorating the house while they slept. Some mornings the paintings would be on different walls or a chair had gone missing because I'd decided it needed to be reupholstered. Even after my children went off to college, they'd joke with me about my evolving décor. During visits home, Amy and Joanie often complained that they couldn't find or recognize their own bedrooms. One year before a big holiday dinner, I moved the dining room into the living room and the living room into the dining room. I'm impulsive, what can I say? I like to put a fresh face on an old room. Or even an old roof. Yes, I once decided I didn't like the color of our roof, so I had it painted black.

"Who paints their roof?" my girlfriend Mary Ann asked with mock disbelief.

"Want me to paint yours?" I replied.

My mother called the impulse to refine or make a space more beautiful "being fussy." Now when I use the word fussy, I don't mean make a fuss, but rather the impulse to pay close attention to details. As I do, Vera wanted everything around her to be perfectly inviting. She believed that the functional and the practical should also be, in some way, lovely. Even her closets were neat and appealing. "Look for ways to put beauty where it doesn't exist," she'd say.

This very colorful way of thinking evolved into one of Vera Bradley's driving principles—we create beautiful solutions—products that are functional and work in your everyday life, and that are also engaging to the eye.

As far back as I can remember, Mother's attention to detail was sharp. She did this to set a mood. Growing up in the house of Vera Bradley, our family dinners were always candlelit (Dad was in the candle business, after all) and Mother never saved the good silver for guests. On nearly every ordinary day she'd have a fresh, homemade cake under the dome because "it looks so pretty." And she'd often match the color of the frosting to the plate. To Vera, presentation was everything. Whatever the situation, she wanted it to be just right for whomever she was hosting, whether that was Dad and our family, or a houseful of guests. (I remember one evening when she searched for an Italian radio station to create just the right atmosphere for our takeout pizza!)

The way Vera fussed over the details always made whoever was in our house feel special, which is probably why there always seemed to be people over. I know it brought her great joy and personal satisfaction, too.

After Dad died, I made a habit of calling Mother at dinnertime because I knew it had become a lonely event for her. Of all those many phone calls, I can't remember a time when she told me what she was actually eating, but she always described how her table was beautifully set for one. There was always a cloth napkin, candles, and freshly cut flowers. I recall one specific conversation where she was so delighted to report, "Barbara, dear, I'm eating off of that darling oval plate with the gold ribbon trim. Remember the one?" Mother was a big proponent for leftovers because, she argued, if

"LOOK FOR WAYS TO PUT BEAUTY WHERE IT DOESN'T EXIST," VERA WOULD SAY. THAT VERY COLORFUL WAY OF THINKING EVOLVED INTO ONE OF VERA BRADLEY'S DRIVING PRINCIPLES—WE CREATE BEAUTIFUL SOLUTIONS.

you put them on a different plate and dressed them up with a little garnish, you can call it a new meal.

I believe anyone can learn to create an inviting ambiance. Once, when my grandson Eddie was not yet five years old, he sat down at my kitchen table for a simple meal of spaghetti and meatballs. "Let's eat," I said as I set down his plate. He looked around at the table and then back up at me with a puzzled expression. "But Birdie, where is the centerpiece?"

Careful consideration of the details creates a richer experience for people, and a more memorable one. A question I often ask myself when I'm reviewing the look, feel, and function of our showrooms and retail spaces, hosting an event at the office, or planning a party in my own home is: what is the experience I want to create? What are the types of memories I want to make for my guests? How can I create a special moment for my customers, friends, or family? What can I shift in the room or improve in the product we're designing to enhance the experience? In other words, how can I be a little more fussy?

The design team at Vera Bradley refers to me as "the great tweaker" or the "chief tweaking officer" because I will zoom in on the details of a product and know instinctively what needs to be tweaked to align with the Vera Bradley brand and our customer. Maybe the shade is slightly off? Perhaps the pattern isn't the right scale? This editorial insight can be a blessing and a curse but mostly I attribute much of the company's success to focusing so strongly on the details and the finishing touches in everything we create.

We have similarly gone to great lengths to create a memorable experience in the Vera Bradley corporate offices. Bold colors and vibrant wallpaper decorate the walls. The furniture is comfortable. Fresh-cut flowers are arranged throughout, and I make a habit of turning on desk lamps and turning off the overhead fluorescents in every room I pass through. The right lighting is a big one for me.

If a lightbulb is out, I notice it immediately, and I have a drawer full of 40-watt bulbs right next to the hammer and nails at both the office and at home to ensure that warm light is a constant. My grandson Chris jokes that the day they invented the dimmer switch was one of my happiest. He's right; it ranks pretty high on my happy list. Second to that is the day they invented an app to turn on all your house lights before you pull into the driveway. Genius!

I understand that I set a high expectation of fussy, and sometimes there's a learning curve. When a woman from our sales department set a luncheon table with paper napkins, plates, and plastic utensils for our visual design specialists, I pulled her aside and said, "These are our *visual design specialists*. Let's pull out the cloth napkins, the china, and the silver flatware and show them how it's done." The best way to communicate the importance we put on the details, after all, is to make a fuss over them ourselves.

I pull out all the stops for our partners and retailers but, most important, I want our office environment to be just right for our employees. I believe that everyone in the company should enjoy beauty down to every last detail—even the bathroom soap. In our New York office, we recently redesigned the restrooms. We enlarged our "Parisian Paisley" print and wallpapered every wall, including the ceiling. It's spectacular and now, going to the restroom always draws comments. In fact, the Vera Bradley board easily recruited its next new member after she used our employee bathroom. This particular woman was impressed, she said, that if we considered the comfort of our employees this much, we must be a very caring company and one she wanted to be a part of. "Count me in!" she said.

You too can learn to notice, and appreciate, the details. Adding a splash of color or beauty doesn't have to be a big project. I tend to do things in a big way, but that's not always necessary. Just keep in mind that when you create a warm environment that invites people in and makes them feel special, they want to return again and again. That's the Vera Bradley way.

WHAT KIND OF SPECIAL MOMENTS CAN YOU CREATE?

YOU'RE *Welcome*

Details matter, so consider the experience you want to create for yourself and others in your life, at home and at work. In what ways can you be a little more "fussy" and redesign your world in a way that creates that sense of home wherever you go?

Are your home and workspace comfortable to you and inviting to others? How can you make them feel more like a home?

REFINE YOUR TASTES

I f a particular aspect of your personal or professional life isn't as comfortable as you'd like, work toward creating an environment that is more appealing to you. Just as we each have individual strengths, we also each have preferred tastes. Do you know what yours are?

Where I can hardly sit through five minutes of the Cooking Channel I can watch HGTV all day long. I'm just not a "foodie." Ask anyone who's dined with me. Or ask Joan Maxwell.

Joan worked for Vera Bradley for twelve years, many of which were spent commuting back and forth between Fort Wayne and San Francisco. Rather than stay in a hotel or get a separate apartment when she was in town, I'd invite her to stay with me in my home. After over a decade of essentially living together, she said to me, "Barb, don't you ever get tired of toast for breakfast?" I opened my refrigerator to reveal a lonely apple, two yogurts, and a carton of milk for our morning coffee.

"Choose anything you like," I said with a wink.

As far as I'm concerned, toast served with jam on a beautiful plate and savored with a good friend is as lovely as it gets, and quite a suitable breakfast, too. You see, for me, the dining experience is about much more than food, it's

EMBRACE AND APPRECIATE YOUR PREFERRED TASTES WITHOUT APOLOGY.

about enjoying the right atmosphere and the right people. In my home, that's what makes a meal. I'd rather set an elaborate table for twelve than choose the menu any day. That's *my* preferred taste.

Whether I'm out to dinner or throwing a dinner party, the bulk of my attention and time goes toward creating an aesthetically memorable experience—beautiful lighting, bright flowers (preferably that match the wallpaper), just the right music, and a great mix of people. My late husband Peer shared my appreciation for striking the right mood. He used to take pictures of my table settings before the guests arrived. Talk about a man after my own heart.

Where food is an element not to be overlooked, I will easily hand the oven mitts over to someone else—a caterer if need be.

Not that that's without its perils.

After one of the last parties I hosted, a man who lives on my floor stopped me in the hallway.

"I didn't know you could play the piano," he said. "How long have you been performing?"

I smiled politely even though I had no idea what he was talking about.

"Oh, don't be modest." He smiled back. "The catering staff told me you're amazing. They heard you play at your last party."

I couldn't help laughing out loud. He was referring to my "performance" at my player piano. You know—the computerized kind that plays on its own? One of my favorite party tricks is to sit down in front of the ivories and pretend-play Cole Porter. The catering staff must have concluded that I was some kind of closet pianist.

I continued to laugh, loving that the thing the catering staff at my party was talking about most was my so-called musicianship. (I wonder what my brother would think of that!)

At the end of the day, I will probably not be remembered for my musical or culinary talents. Unless, of course, it's for my sautéed onions. Before starting Vera Bradley, to convince my first husband that I could care for our four children, manage our home, and juggle my side job, I used to race home before him, wash the wallpaper paste off my hands and quickly sauté onions in butter to make the house smell as if I'd been cooking all day. A cute trick, isn't it? And it worked. Plus, the truth is that in those days when my children were young, I actually did cook. And quite a bit. But now I live alone, and I put my energy into other things. Today, my tastes lie elsewhere. That's what makes me, me.

A MATTER OF *Taste*

In addition to identifying your strengths, define your unique tastes. Ask
yourself what you love to do, and where you'd prefer to put your energy.
We all have things we love and others not so much. I make a habit of
embracing and appreciating my tastes without apology. You can honor
your unique tastes and still be gracious around others who have different
preferences.

DEFINE YOUR STYLE

I'm well into my seventies and I love to wear skinny jeans and a skirt above the knee. Why not? I trust that my daughters will tell me when they think I should give it up. (*Hint hint,* I trust that they will.)

Not too many years ago, my granddaughter Molly participated in Spirit Week at Homestead High School, where she and her friends were to dress up for "senior citizen day." I was proud to be her model; unfortunately dressing like me didn't get her credit for participation. "It was *senior citizen* day," her teacher scolded, "and you came dressed in skinny jeans and heels." Molly promptly pulled out her phone and searched for my photo. "This is my grandmother." Enough said.

I wear what I wear not to set trends or make a fashion statement, but to define my own style. I similarly encourage everyone at the office to wear what they feel good in. On any given day, the range of styles at the Vera Bradley offices in both Fort Wayne and Manhattan swing from H&M to Chanel with everything in between. At one point our human resources director suggested we enact a dress

I BELIEVE THAT EVERYONE HAS HIS OR HER OWN PERSONAL STYLE AND THAT DEFINING IT—AND DEFENDING IT!—IS RIGHT UP THERE WITH THE REST OF OUR PERSONAL RIGHTS.

code for our predominantly female staff. I said, "I don't believe in dictated fashion. I want to see what women are wearing." Vera Bradley creates looks for girls and women ages eight to eighty. We're not a one-size-fits-all brand and that's because there's not one size, trend, or style that fits all women. In other words, I don't believe in dressing to fit in, which is why we create a range of looks to reflect the colorful lifestyles of the women who carry us. Backpacks for campus, totes for the office, and wristlets for happy hour.

I believe that everyone has his or her own personal style and that defining it—and defending it!—is right up there with the rest of our personal rights. Besides, most people know the difference between what's appropriate and what isn't. For those who don't, their style is interesting to me, too. It's watching the parade of fashion throughout the office and outside on the street that inspires new Vera Bradley designs, and also allows me to develop and refine my own look, which I'd call classic and casually on-trend. I love to mix prints and patterns with all washes of denim—white, black, blue, and gray. My jewelry tends to be the time-honored variety—gold hoops or diamond studs—and then I like to throw on a bangle or something colorful from the Vera Bradley collection for fun. I'm also known for adding a patterned scarf to call an outfit "done."

One Halloween, the Vera Bradley staff came dressed as me—redheaded wigs, navy check blouses, jeans, and patterned scarves. Boy, they know me well! On most days, this is my uniform. Although I'm always open to mixing it up or adding a splash of something new.

While I travel with the design team to London, Paris, and other fashion centers around the world to study the latest in emerging trends, I actually learn more about fashion by simply studying what real women wear Monday through Friday. An updated rendition of the traditional kimono may draw gasps on a runway during fashion week, but it doesn't necessarily work at the office or meeting a girlfriend for lunch. Unless, of course, she crops it, belts it, or somehow makes it her own.

To those who say women should "dress their age," I say—ridiculous! What does that even mean, anyway? We each determine for ourselves what is age-appropriate based on what feels and looks good on our bodies. Don't let your age determine what you wear. Rather, let your level of comfort and confidence determine how you dress for the day. Take pride in your look. After all, you created it. It's uniquely yours. And if it's not, consider whose look you're wearing. Have you fallen into the label trap? It can be easy to do, but just because it's in the Saks Fifth Avenue window doesn't mean it's going to work on you. Designer labels and price point don't dictate what I wear. I may wear an Hermès jacket one day, and a blouse from fast-fashion retailer Zara the next. (In fact, my favorite skirt is from Zara because it's the perfect fit.) Everyone who's ever shopped with me knows that I trust my eye and I buy pieces that work on my body and complement my particular style. Period.

I consider it a high compliment that my twenty-four-year-old granddaughter Frannie asks to borrow my clothes. In fact, we often buy off the same rack. We've been on a shoe kick of late, and Frannie recently walked into my New York apartment in a pair I recognized. "I just bought those in blue!" I exclaimed.

"Really? Mom thought they were too indulgent."

"No—they're fabulous."

> DON'T LET YOUR AGE DETERMINE WHAT YOU WEAR. RATHER, LET YOUR COMFORT AND CONFIDENCE DETERMINE HOW YOU DRESS FOR THE DAY.

While I delight endlessly in Frannie's approval and emulation of my style—I mean, there's a fifty-year age difference between us—and while our company designs for the current times, what I've learned is that it's not necessarily the younger generations that set trends. I used to think that mothers borrowed fashion inspiration from their daughters but in my case, it was the other way around. My mother worked as a Vera Bradley sales rep in Miami Beach until she passed away, and she was setting trends even after she died.

At the time of Mother's funeral, the company was still designing apparel, so as we prepared for her open-casket service for friends and family, I chose a new Vera Bradley outfit in a floral pattern we hadn't yet introduced. I just knew she would have loved it. Well, she was nearly as beautiful after she passed on as she was in life, and when one of Mother's devoted customers and friends approached her casket I heard a gasp followed by, "Is that the *new blue*?" I'd wanted to present Mother in something pretty, but I hadn't intended on premiering the new pattern at her funeral! Mother was still selling even after her death. That was *her* style and it never got old.

OWN IT!

When you clearly define your style—the look and attitude that makes *you* feel the most comfortable and you wear it with confidence—you make a lasting impression at any age. Have you defined your personal and professional style? Do you "own it," as my granddaughters like to say? Just like with any other future choice you make for your life and your work, it's never too late—or too early—to refine or even redesign your style entirely.

KEEP MOVING & ALLOW FOR LITTLE EXTRAS

At my age, I move faster than most people I know. I'm frequently asked, "Where do you get your energy?" My answer is, "I don't stop moving long enough to slow down." My children will agree with this. They say I've been going a hundred miles per hour since they were little kids. They love to tell the story of the time I had all four of them, including our family dog, in the station wagon when a helicopter started trailing me on the highway. The kids were all saying, "Mom, there's a helicopter chasing us—pull over!" "He's not following *us*," I insisted. But then, after we'd traveled several miles and it was still hovering above us and a police car appeared in my rearview mirror with its siren on, I relented and pulled over.

"What the heck are you doing?" the officer said. "Didn't you see that chopper waving you to pull over?"

"Me—what for?" I asked innocently.

"For *speeding*. Ma'am, you were driving well over the speed limit. You need to slow down."

STAYING YOUTHFUL AND LIVELY IS A MIND-SET.

Slowing down just isn't one of my strengths. I need to move. Mother was the same way, so perhaps high energy is inherited—part of your DNA. I do also believe in positive thinking. Staying youthful and lively is a mind-set. You'll rarely hear me complain about being too tired, too this or too that. My attitude is to keep moving, and I'm known for encouraging those around me to match my momentum. For example, I'm always inviting out-of-town friends and coworkers to stay with me, but most of them get their own hotel room because they complain that I stay up too late. "With Barb," they say, "it's always a late night." Last summer, my granddaughter Frannie stayed with me in my New York apartment for a month and was often surprised when she tiptoed in well past midnight and I'd still be awake—and usually entertaining friends.

My late husband, Peer, was my equal in vitality and drive, and he was fifteen years older than me. It wasn't unusual for us to meet up for a late dinner in New York after both working long days at our separate offices. We liked to go to Marie's Crisis in the West Village after a Broadway show and sing along with the patrons (Peer had the voice and I knew all the words, so together we were in perfect tune), and we'd finally retreat home at an hour that most consider morning. I remember the time he had cataract surgery and his doctors instructed him to go straight home, take a nap, and rest. He turned to me and lowered his voice, "Now, I'm not getting into *that* habit."

I've never adopted that habit, either.

The real secret to staying vibrant, I think, is engaging in life, putting yourself in stimulating environments, and surrounding yourself with people of all ages who are similarly energized. Or who can, at least, appreciate your level of energy.

Last year, I spoke to my granddaughter Molly's sorority about female entrepreneurship and after my talk, the housemother politely asked me, "Ms. Baekgaard, would you like to take a few minutes to put your feet up? I can set you up in one of the spare bedrooms if you'd like." Before I could answer, Molly spoke for me, "Birdie doesn't put her feet up."

My daily exercise routine is walking up and down the stairs of the Vera Bradley Design Center. My son Tommy once bought me a Fitbit to track my steps. I wore it for about a week and finally took it off because it clashed with my jewelry. But in a week's time of wearing it I averaged the equivalent of five miles a day. When I'm working in New York, my energy goes into hyperdrive. It's not unusual for me to walk nine to ten miles in city blocks a day. I set a zealous pace, especially on Fifth Avenue, and people have a hard time keeping up with me. I remember when my granddaughter Maggie, who was nine years old at the time, complained loudly after trailing behind me for several blocks, "Birdie, you walk too fast." I laughed and said, "Remember that when you're my age."

Two years ago, I broke my foot and it took me six weeks before I realized something was wrong. I still don't know how it happened (I must have stepped off a curb the wrong way), but I kept walking on it until it started to swell and I reluctantly went to the doctor. He looked at me like I had three heads and put my foot in a boot right then and there. Thankfully it was fall in New York—perfect boot weather.

When you're focused on fun and engaging in life, it's easy to ignore a little foot pain. This is not to say that you shouldn't take care of yourself. I may often be operating in overdrive, but I'm not reckless. I know when I need to stop. I won't forget the time a fifty-five-year-old woman suffered a mild heart attack while waiting in line to purchase several bags of discounted products at the Vera Bradley outlet sale. This annual sale in Fort Wayne attracts up to sixty-five thousand

THE REAL SECRET TO STAYING VIBRANT IS ENGAGING IN LIFE, PUTTING YOURSELF IN STIMULATING ENVIRONMENTS, AND SURROUNDING YOURSELF WITH PEOPLE OF ALL AGES WHO ARE SIMILARLY ENERGIZED.

Vera-philes from all over the country to sift through over nine hundred thousand pieces of discounted product so, needless to say, the checkout lines can be long. As the woman slumped to the ground, the shoppers around her immediately came to her aid and attracted the attention of a Vera Bradley worker, who called an ambulance. But when the paramedics showed up, she didn't want to go. She protested losing her place in line. I completely understand not wanting to lose a good deal, but she was having a heart attack! At some point, we each have to recognize when we're pushing ourselves too far. She finally relented to receive care when a Vera Bradley outlet worker promised to deliver her items to her hospital room. (And he did, in a pink bag.)

I understand that preserving energy and vibrancy means daily self-care. This looks different for everyone, so it's important to figure out what care looks like for *you*. My routine is very much my own and it comes at the end of the day. After I've watched an hour of the late-night television host Jimmy Fallon, I wash my face with a hearty dollop of coconut oil and slip into a hot sea-salt bath for twenty minutes. This is when I let any stress from the day dissolve in the bath and drain away. This is my tried-and-true prescription for a good night's rest and replenishing my energy for the next day.

Anyone who's traveled with me knows that if I get put in a hotel room that doesn't have a bathtub, I'll ask to be moved to one that does. It's nonnegotiable. This might sound a little spoiled or, I don't know—demanding—and if it does, I'm okay with that. I believe that we must each find ways to spoil ourselves, to allow and sometimes even demand for ourselves a little something extra every day. My nightly bath routine is my little extra.

INDULGE THE "EXTRAS"

What's your little extra? Is it a long soak in a tub, a short walk after dinner, or a few quiet moments of meditation in the morning? How do you take care of yourself from day to day? If daily self-care isn't on your to-do list, or you worry it's too indulgent, think of that little something extra as your key to productivity and an overall sense of richness in your life.

MAKE YUM YUM CAKE

My daughter Joanie was turning one when I was nine months pregnant with my second child. I'd planned a small birthday party for her, and I'd made Vera's Yum Yum Cake—basic white cake with Cool Whip and vanilla pudding frosting. Simple and very yummy. But a few hours before the birthday guests were to arrive, I started feeling a little queasy. I was sure I wasn't going into labor quite yet, but my friend and neighbor who was helping me with the party insisted I go to my obstetrician's office—just in case. Well, one look at me, and my doctor said, "You're having a baby!"

"Not today," I protested, "I'm having a *party*."

Despite my insistence that I return home in time to cut the cake, I was admitted to the hospital where my second daughter, Amy, was born within hours. The following year on November 13, I threw a much bigger party to celebrate the sisters who share a birthday.

There was always a reason

to celebrate in the Bradley household.

Vera with her sister Bonnie.

That notion of making Yum Yum Cake—taking the time to celebrate—is a personal and professional value. In fact, marking a celebration is often the order of the day in the Vera Bradley offices. Baby showers, weddings, anniversaries, birthdays, and graduations—we celebrate them all. I don't like to let a big moment go by without celebrating it. Suffice to say, we eat a lot of cake.

When Vera was still alive and all her children were grown, she used to tease that Dad always enjoyed a big birthday celebration while she never did. "No one comes for my birthday," she'd tease. Well, there was a reason for that. Dad's birthday was in February and hers was in August. While we all welcomed a February escape to their sunny Miami Beach home, no one wanted to travel to Florida in the heat of late summer. So in 2009, to honor what would have been Vera's hundredth birthday, we celebrated in all of the three thousand stores that carry Vera Bradley. To commemorate her big day, we sent out formal party invitations inviting customers to receive a free gift plus special promotions on their favorite products, along with celebratory cupcakes and punch. The event was such a huge success that now we celebrate Vera's birthday every year. August 9 has become one of the most anticipated shopping days on the Vera Bradley calendar. Every time it rolls around, I laugh to myself. *Well, Mother, are you happy now? Now everyone celebrates your birthday.*

In the early days of the company, we started giving every employee a fifty-dollar bill for his or her birthday with a handwritten card stating, *This is to be spent on you.* The gesture was meant to make the recipient feel special, and to communicate that you are more than an employee. You are family and we celebrate you. Today, with nearly three thousand employees company wide, we still give everyone a fifty-dollar bill in a card on his or her birthday. Every year our finance

DON'T LET A BIG MOMENT GO BY WITHOUT CELEBRATING IT. AND WHILE YOU'RE AT IT, WHY NOT CELEBRATE THE SMALL MOMENTS, TOO!

department asks if we can just roll the money into people's paychecks, and I continue to say no. When you receive money in cash, it's just more meaningful. Besides, this little gift is meant as "fun money" to buy something for themselves, not to pay the cable bill or buy groceries.

Our vice president of product design and development, Veronique Poudrier, began working at Vera Bradley within a month of her birthday and when she came into the office to discover her desk decorated with confetti, streamers, flowers, and balloons on her big day, she broke down in tears. She later confided in me that for the nearly fifteen years she'd worked at her last job, her birthday had never once been acknowledged. "I don't think my boss ever even knew when my birthday was," she said.

CELEBRATE AND ELEVATE

Whether it's your birthday or just an ordinary Wednesday, I believe we should each challenge ourselves to find ways to celebrate and elevate the every day. What's your perfect day? My dream day would start by waking up at my lake cottage in Indiana surrounded by my family and end later that night in New York City with girlfriends attending a Broadway play. Since this schedule isn't really practical within a twenty-four-hour window, I look for simpler ways to elevate my every day. As a daily practice I look for ways to add color, humor, and surprise, along with some combination of family and good friends. Every day is worth celebrating. How can you incorporate elements of your perfect day into your tomorrow?

CULTIVATE NEW FRIENDSHIPS

My seventy-fifth birthday might have been my best. I was in New York for a board meeting and while I hadn't made any big plans to celebrate, I was perfectly happy just to be in my favorite city. Really, in New York all you have to do is walk out your front door and you'll get swept up in some kind of party. I'd stopped home after a day at the office when I heard the doorbell. When I opened it I was shocked to see my four children *and* their spouses, along with my sister Joan, Gregory Philpotts, and my dear friends Glenna and Mary Ann screaming, "Surprise!"

They took me to see the then off-Broadway play, *Disaster!* featuring one of my favorite playwrights and actors, Seth Rudetsky. I've been a Broadway addict since the days when Dad would visit me at Marymount College and take me to whatever play we could get day-of tickets for. Over the years, I've seen dozens of performances, many of them featuring Seth, so seeing his newest play on my birthday was a huge gift in itself. But when Seth and fifteen cast members arrived at my apartment after the show with a dozen roses for *me*, I thought I must have already died and gone to heaven. My family and friends had brought the backstage party to me! *How in the world had they pulled this off?* I never did find out. Nor did I question it because it was probably the single most fun evening of my life. Talk about elevating the every day. It doesn't get much higher than that.

Except it did.

My seventy-fifth birthday surprise became the gift that kept giving. After that wonderful night, Seth and I became great friends. I soon met his adorable husband, James, and their daughter, Juli, and they welcomed me into their Broadway community where I've met some of the most talented and humble people in the world—and also the happiest, I suspect, because they're doing what they love. This new texture to my life was so unexpected and has become the source of much laughter, color, and joy. The Broadway acting community knows how to keep the *f* in fun, no doubt about it, and they like to keep the same late-night hours as I do. And since I love a good party and will make any excuse to have one, I host many parties for my new friends. In fact, on the final night of *Disaster!* on Broadway, I invited the entire cast back to my apartment. Seth played my piano (and he *really* knows how to play) and we all sang well into the morning light.

THE *Gift* OF FRIENDSHIP

Be willing to expand your social group—both inside and outside the home and office—to include relationships that shift the current design of your life. New friendships can often inspire positive changes. Who have you met lately who energizes you and adds a new splash of color to your days? How can you take steps to welcome new relationships into your life that elevate your experience?

Color

Your

Life

FIND YOUR BALANCE

C an women have it all? Can we have a career, a family, friendships, and time for ourselves? The answer is yes—but not all at once. And only if we reconsider how much we can balance in a single day with what we can juggle over the course of our lives.

I feel like I've achieved a balance in my life—*over time,* Some might say that my first marriage failed because of my career. It's true that my husband's mantra had always been "fifty and out" and indeed, as soon as he turned fifty, he did declare himself ready to retire on the beach in Florida. While sitting beachside may sound like paradise to many, I wasn't ready for that. Vera Bradley was growing and I wanted to grow with it.

Did I choose work over marriage? At that point in my life, I guess I did. At other periods in my life, however, my creativity and passions were put on the back burner because I was raising four children and family was my top priority. Similarly, I can recount years when my attention toward my children came second to the needs of my closest friendships. When my dear friend Mary Sloane was dying from breast cancer, she occupied my thoughts and I visited her home in Virgina whenever possible. So, yes, there have been times when I felt that things were out

CAN WE HAVE A CAREER, A FAMILY, FRIENDSHIPS, AND TIME FOR OURSELVES? THE ANSWER IS YES—BUT NOT ALL AT ONCE.

of balance, but when I look at my life overall, I feel as if it's evened out pretty well.

That I'd learned to strike a balance over the years was clear to me when Vera Bradley premiered the "Disney Parks" collection. It's not every day your company designs accessories and bags featuring Mickey and Minnie Mouse, so I thought it would be fun to take my then high-school-age granddaughter Maggie with me to Disney World near Orlando. When we arrived at the store for the grand opening, there was a spiraling line of eight hundred people who had been waiting all morning to get into the store. Before I could catch my breath, I was ushered inside where I was crowded by Disney tourists eager for me to autograph their new Vera Bradley bags. At one point, an enthusiastic woman with her daughter in tow turned to Maggie and asked, "What's it like to have a celebrity as a grandmother?" Totally unaware of my so-called status, Maggie looked at her with confusion. Finally, she shyly shrugged her shoulders because to her, I'm just Birdie. I smiled at her, realizing that even with all the time I give to my career, my grandchildren see a different side of me—the grandmother, mother, sister, and friend.

At Vera Bradley we design products for women who feel pulled in many directions—the woman who's trying her best to do good in the world and also take care of her kids, her special friendships, and of course herself. Since our design team is predominantly women, we really do get it. We often sit around the office and talk about the challenge of striking that delicate day-to-day and overall life balance. My intention has always been to create a working environment that allows for an easier work-life equilibrium. Just as I've done in my own life, I encourage everyone who works for Vera Bradley to create a healthy balance and if I notice that someone is struggling, I'll sometimes step in. "Go home and be with your family," I might say. "Take a personal day or a long weekend." "Commit to leaving the office at five o'clock." While I can appreciate working long and late because you love the work you do (I do so frequently myself), I believe that at the end of the day you probably won't regret spending fewer hours at the office, but you will regret not tucking your children into bed.

As I've shared throughout these pages, some of my fondest memories are of my grandchildren. I can't imagine having missed out on any of them. Not the time my grandson Christopher kissed me good-bye on my front porch and lost his first tooth, and certainly not the countless weekends over the summers when I've made my famous waffles at our lake house for my grandchildren and their friends, and friends of their friends. I've sometimes had to juggle three waffle irons at a time. (Sixty-five waffles in one morning is my personal best!) I'll never forget the time when my then three-year-old granddaughter Audrey sat by my side as I whipped up another bowl of batter.

"And now for my secret ingredient," I whispered to her. "I put soda water in the batter. Makes them extra crispy."

"My daddy has a secret when he makes waffles, too," she whispered back.

"Oh, what is it?" I asked.

"He uses a toaster."

If I had created a life for myself where my long hours at work stole moments like these, I'd have missed out on making memories I wouldn't be able to create later. That's a regret I don't want to have.

When interviewing Beatrice MacCabe to lead our design team, she nervously announced to me that she was expecting her third baby. She said something like, "I just found out I'm pregnant and I understand if I can't secure this job." She worried that she might lose the opportunity to work at

YOU PROBABLY WON'T REGRET SPENDING FEWER HOURS AT THE OFFICE, BUT YOU WILL REGRET NOT TUCKING YOUR CHILDREN INTO BED.

Vera Bradley if she asked for twelve weeks maternity leave so soon after starting. While it might be the attitude in other corporate environments to discriminate against mothers and working parents, it's certainly not ours. Our feeling is that you should never be afraid to tell your employer that you're pregnant, or that you have a graduation or a school performance to attend. In fact, we love it when people share this type of news; it's usually accompanied by a big cheer throughout the building. I gave Beatrice a hug and said, "That's just wonderful." We offered her the position. We wanted her—and her baby.

What I've discovered over the years is that when you acknowledge and respect your employees for having multidimensional lives, when you understand that they are *more* than their job, they give back the extra hours when necessary—often without being asked. This is especially true of mothers. In fact, (cover your ears, HR), in my experience, I find that mothers are often stronger and more efficient workers because they know better how to prioritize, multitask, and balance the demands of their job with their responsibilities at home. Who wouldn't value this skill set?

I remember once accompanying Vera and my special needs brother, Jamie, to the doctor's office. Back then there were no handicap parking spots, and no ramps to assist in getting a disabled child from a car and into a building. Jamie was about fourteen at the time, and helplessly dead weight. I watched in awe as my five-foot-five mother lifted this nearly full-grown child out of the car. It occurred to me in that moment how many times she must have done this over the years, and how difficult it must have been. And yet, Vera never complained. She never even mentioned these trips. Caring for Jamie in this way was just one of the many things she juggled.

As I watched Mother carry my brother across the parking lot, I had a new appreciation for how well she seemed to do it all. She balanced an especially

IF YOU PUT YOUR ATTENTION WHERE IT'S NEEDED IN THE MOMENT, YOUR LIFE WILL BALANCE OUT OVER TIME.

challenging child and five others who were demanding in their own ways. She balanced a marriage and close friendships—plus, she maintained a beautiful household and entertained regularly. How *did* she do it all? She didn't do it all at once. She put her attention where it was needed in the moment, and over time her life balanced out beautifully.

LIFE IS A BALANCING ACT

Sometimes our life's priorities are crystal clear. At other times we have to make a choice about what we're going to focus on just for today and hope the other things can wait. My habit is to make a mental list every night in the tub. I check off what I did, knowing that what didn't make the list today can wait its turn until tomorrow—or another day after that.

While it's tempting to try and do it all, the truth is that we simply cannot do it all at once. Life is a balancing act where what's most important is how we spend our energy and attention *over time*, rather than over the course of *one* day.

FOLLOW LOVE

I distinctly remember the moment I set eyes on my second husband, Peer. I'd been nominated by Will Little to serve on the board of directors for the Chicago gift show and it was my first meeting. I came straight from our booth at McCormick Place and walked into the event room at the top of the John Hancock Center in my Vera Bradley one-size-fits-all skirt and matching camisole. Peer was standing among a group of men on the opposite side of the room, and as I watched him carry on, laughing and holding court, I wondered, *Who is this tall, handsome, and impeccably dressed man with a buzz all around him?* Turns out, he was the president of the board! Peer captured my attention as he led the meeting that night. I sat happily through every minute of it. And remember, I don't like meetings.

Afterward, Peer approached me and politely explained that it was tradition for the board president to take out its newest members for a drink. Although skeptical about this "board protocol," I was enchanted nevertheless. I accepted his offer.

We then joined Vera and my sister Joan at the Whitehall Hotel bar. After a round of drinks and lively conversation, he graciously said good night. Mother

LOVE HAS A WAY OF CAPTURING YOUR ATTENTION.

turned to me with curiosity. "How long have you known Peer?"

"We just met today."

"Well." She gave me a wry smile. "He looks at you like he could eat you with a spoon."

Mother was a romantic at heart and she noticed our instant chemistry. Peer and I just clicked. There was no denying the sparks between us, not to mention the mutual passion we shared for the gift industry. Peer owned a men's gift-import business, so he appreciated what Pat and I were building with Vera Bradley. He quickly became a cheerleader for the brand—I'd later joke that I got him "wholesale."

Mother also picked up on something I'd noticed, too: Peer's resemblance to Dad. Both men were kind, charismatic, secure in their own skin, self-made, and successful. Everyone loved Ed Bradley and it was the same with Peer. At six foot three and with a Danish accent, his charm and easy humor had a way of drawing you in. Mother used to tease with a wink, "Peer may be fifteen years older than you but he's only fifteen years younger than me." Peer and Ed Bradley both stood out in a crowd and I believe it's no coincidence that the very year Dad died was the same year Peer entered my life.

I was forty-eight and Peer was sixty-three when we met. Our courtship was the old-fashioned—before texting—kind. I lived and worked in Fort Wayne and he in a suburb of Chicago, so we sent handwritten love letters back and forth to each other until we were able to meet up again at the next gift show or take a business trip together. Peer liked to say that if you travel or go on vacation with someone and when you get home you don't want to say good-bye, that's the barometer for enduring love. Peer always said he wanted one more day together. I wish for that, too.

But because we each had viable companies in different cities, we kept our separate homes for fifteen years (perhaps *that's* the key to enduring love), traveling back and forth between Fort Wayne and Northbrook, Illinois, on the weekends until we

With my adorable husband, Peer.

LOVE IS THAT FEELING OF ALWAYS WANTING ONE MORE DAY TOGETHER.

eventually bought an apartment in downtown Chicago. It was the perfect setup. At least, it worked for us. When Peer asked me to marry him, he gave me a gold ring with a leopard print design. He had been single for fourteen years before he met me, so when he slipped it onto my finger, he said, "Because you changed my spots."

But the truth is that Peer changed me more than I changed him. The lyrics of "For Good" from *Wicked* say it perfectly: "Because I knew you, I have been changed for good." Peer really did change me for the better because, to my eye, he was the embodiment of good. I admired how he conducted himself in every way. To me, there wasn't a facet of his life he couldn't be proud of. He'd come over to this country from Denmark after serving in the Danish resistance in World War II. After enduring a POW camp and the great hardships of war, he was determined to remake himself in America and have the life he'd always dreamed of. That's exactly what Peer did. He welcomed every day with appreciation and no matter where or whom he was with, Peer was gracious, engaging—and always a whole lot of fun.

In my midfifties, I got a second chance at marriage and I couldn't believe my luck. I *still* can't believe it. Whenever people refer to me as a "widow," I'm taken aback. I don't see myself under a veil of grief. I miss Peer every day, but more than anything, I just feel lucky to have found him and enjoyed him for as long as I did. I remember coming home from parties and just the two of us dancing to Frank Sinatra's "The Way You Look Tonight." Peer would say, "There wasn't a better-looking woman in the room tonight," and I'd reply, "And you were the most handsome man." And we believed it. I used to joke, "We're like that couple in the movie, *The Enchanted Cottage*." I'm referring to the 1945 classic where a homely maid and a scarred ex-GI meet at the cottage where she works and they fall in love. While they were unattractive to the outside world, they were beautiful to each other. It was similar with us. Wherever we were, Peer and I only had eyes for each other. He was the dashing Dane and I was his tall redhead. When I think back to those magical moments, I want to freeze them. They remain some of my most dear. My good friend Glenna remarked once, "Peer acts like you hung the moon." She's right, he absolutely did and I was equally dazzled by him. Peer lit up a room like a thousand stars.

CHOOSE LOVE

Who has changed you for the good? Who inspires you to be a better version of yourself—a better friend, partner, sister, or mother? I believe we each have people on our "life's" board of directors—who is on yours? In my experience, when you follow love—that is, when you surround yourself with positive people who give you a charge and bring out your own greatness—your life will light up and expand in directions you never imagined possible.

REMEMBER ROMANCE

Peer and I loved to unwind after a long day by going out for a martini and dinner. I always order my martinis straight up with ice on the side. While I actually prefer my martini on the rocks, I like the long stem of the martini glass rather than the short, stubby glass. Nothing's prettier, so to my mind this is a beautiful solution and an important detail.

We'd always make dinner reservations for three. This was our little trick, so that we'd be seated side by side at a four-top instead of sitting across from each other at a skinny table for two. Peer and I liked to sit close. It's more romantic that way. (And it wasn't totally dishonest. We never knew when a friend might show up and take a seat.)

I gained an appreciation for romance by watching Mother and Dad. They always appeared so much in love, and even with six children they made time for each other—to play golf, go out to dinner, or just sit on the porch and laugh. Dad would often travel for six weeks at a time with Victory Light Candles, and on the day he was due to return home, Mother would make sure it was a big event. The whole family would be waiting for him on the train platform, and then we'd go home to enjoy a special dinner that Vera had prepared to celebrate Dad's home-coming.

Mother and Dad always made marriage look easy, and to the very end they were romantics. Dad passed away in 1987 and Mother five years later on the eve of what would have been their fifty-seventh wedding anniversary. I thought it was sweet and also kind of romantic that they'd be together again on their special day. Of course marriage isn't always romantic, nor is it easy. But I never saw the hard side of it by watching Mother and Dad so I was devastated when my first marriage didn't work out. But then later when I met Peer and got a second chance, I understood their easy love. I finally had it, too.

MAKE ROOM FOR ROMANCE

Taking time for romance is as important as paying the bills, so don't skip it. When you appreciate and celebrate your loved ones—and feel their attention in return—your life will be much more colorful and enchanting.

CELEBRATE YOUR PLACE IN THE WORLD

My late husband, Peer, was just seventeen years old when he joined the Danish Underground in 1940, helping Jews flee to freedom during World War II. He was eventually captured by the Nazis and shipped by train to a prisoner of war camp where he was sentenced to die. Peer endured conditions I cannot fathom—little food, battle planes constantly flying overhead, fear for his life, and an everyday yearning for the simple things like a washcloth and soap. One day, Peer and a few of his fellow prisoners noticed that the front gates of the camp were open. They wondered if their captors were trying to trick them, but they took the opportunity to escape anyhow, hiding in fields and brush as they made the long journey from Germany back home to Copenhagen. By the time they arrived, they learned that the war was over. It was 1945. They'd been liberated.

After the war, Peer enrolled in an exchange-student program that brought him to the University of Washington in Seattle. He returned to Denmark after his studies ended, but was determined to immigrate to America. In 1951, Peer

EXPRESS GRATITUDE FOR THE LIFE YOU BUILD. DON'T TAKE ANYTHING FOR GRANTED.

boarded a ship with all the money he had—one hundred and twenty-seven dollars. After a long week in steerage he arrived in the U.S., ready to start his new life. Peer liked to tell the story of how, after he arrived in New York, he walked into a bar and observed how American men dressed. Those he considered to be "successful businessmen," were those he wanted to emulate. *That's how I need to look,* he told himself.

When I met Peer in the 1980s he was an impeccably dressed and successful businessman running Baekgaard Ltd., a company that imported men's gifts and accessories. Peer had become an American citizen, and though he had lived in this country for thirty years, he never lost his sense of appreciation for the freedom and riches he'd gained. In fact, he'd often remark to me in the grocery store, "Just look at those oranges. Imagine what someone in a third-world country would think to see all of this?" Peer's daily expression of gratitude for the life he built for himself helped me to appreciate what I sometimes took for granted.

Every day I spent with him, Peer taught me how to be a better American. "Claim your heritage," he'd tell me. "Be proud of your country." Denmark was one of the few countries that stood up to the Nazis during World War II. Peer was proud of that and he never expressed any regret for fighting with the resistance despite his capture. As long as I knew him, Peer's Danish heritage was a solid pillar of who he was. It grounded him. And yet, at the same time, he embraced being an American. Truly, I've never met anyone who paid their taxes with more enthusiasm or who marked every voting day on his calendar. He considered it a true misuse of our freedom to miss it.

Peer was lying in his hospital bed the day he died. He hadn't spoken for several days and his doctors and I feared we would soon lose him. I was sitting right next to him, holding his hand when the track on the CD player changed. As the Mormon Tabernacle Choir began singing their rendition of "God Bless America," Peer slowly and quietly began to sing along with them. He never opened his eyes, but he continued to sing every word with absolute clarity through to the very last note. To me, this was his final expression of gratitude to this country, and for the life he dreamed of and was eventually able to create.

To me, Peer's urging to "claim your heritage" can mean more broadly to honor wherever it is you come from, along with the experiences, challenges, and triumphs you've had until now. And from there, to give yourself permission and the freedom to embrace where you're going next—whether that be a new home, a new work environment, a new relationship, or an entirely new version of yourself. Peer was a perfect example of this. He was a man who never lost touch with his heritage, but who embraced fully the opportunities that this country—and this life—gave him to start again.

HONOR YOUR EXPERIENCE

Take a moment to appreciate the richness of your life. We all have something to be proud of and grateful for. Honor where you came from—the experiences, challenges, accomplishments, and people that have made your life what it is today—and from this point forward, make a decision about where you want your life to take you next. You don't have to throw away your past to become the next version of yourself. Stay true to the past, present, and future you.

DISCONTINUE OLD PATTERNS

At Vera Bradley, we're constantly adding more color. That's our thing. In 2006, we were playing around with a standard floral paisley design of pink and brown when we noticed an emerging trend in turquoise, so we swapped out the pink for the blue. We weren't totally sold on the new coloration, but when everyone who walked by the design room stopped to admire it, we reconsidered—*maybe we've landed on something here!* Because the color combination was so different from what we'd done in the past, the sales team encouraged us to order a limited run. Well, the pattern—"Java Blue"—was a huge hit. Our customers were crazy about it and the calls for more were almost unmanageable.

We had never experienced that level of demand for a single pattern, and our initial limited run had to be quickly expanded to fill the flood of orders. If every company has a tipping point, Java Blue was ours. It was *the* pattern that put Vera Bradley in the hands of women all over the map. Suddenly, Java Blue was everywhere.

WHY NOT TRY SOMETHING NEW? YOUR NEXT THING COULD BE YOUR NEXT BIG THING. ISN'T IT WORTH TAKING A RISK?

After the breakout success of this design we began challenging ourselves to think a little bit more outside the paisley lines. We'd learned from this experience that it was worth the risk to push our designs beyond the familiar and expected. We started adding brighter colors to the line and enlarging the scale on some of our prints. Some of our more traditional retailers questioned this bold and bright change but our attitude was: why not try something new? You don't always know what will work until *it works*.

That's the same posture I take in my own life. In order to stay relevant, I believe that individuals, as well as products, companies, and brands, must be open to change. Personally, this excites me. I'm always looking forward, keeping my eyes open for big and small ways to make changes that will redesign my life.

Reflecting back at that pivotal moment in the Atlanta airport in 1982, I didn't realize that I was embarking on a personal redesign. I simply thought Pat and I were acting on a fun idea to create a product that we would enjoy making and that women would delight in carrying. But, in hindsight, I did want a change. And no doubt about it: starting the company was one of the biggest turning points in my life.

I know from speaking with thousands of women since creating Vera Bradley that not everyone embraces change like I do. While I'll fearlessly turn my home upside down and redecorate without a second thought, some women are afraid even to change their hairstyle. I look back at pictures from the 1980s and think: *thank God I stopped teasing my hair*. And shoulder pads—what was I thinking? But that was the style then. It was right for the time.

Strike a bold posture.

Here I am, the future "Tweaker in Chief," at age five.

Around the Vera Bradley design table, there are a few questions we often ask ourselves: Are our collections right for the time? Are we contemporary and current? Or are we stuck in old patterns?

Fashion is a delicate weave of the past, present, and future. We don't want to change so much that we lose our heritage look—the identity that's created a sisterhood of loyal customers throughout the world. Nevertheless, I value those on the creative team who gently push the company forward. If we only stay rooted in the past, they advise, we don't give our customers a reason to buy something new. I agree with this, and again, this point can be applied to our very lives.

When we aren't open to changing our views, taking chances, and moving forward, we run the risk of becoming disinterested, uninspired, or feeling stuck in our lives. We also miss out on countless opportunities. So my question to you, is: when you look at your life today, is it right for the time? Are you staying relevant? Does your current life reflect the life you "see" for yourself? If not, can you discontinue some old patterns to seize new opportunities? Where can you make a change?

At forty-three, I redesigned my life in a big way. I discontinued my pattern of being a stay-at-home mom to pursue the first career of my lifetime. Since then, I've continued to tweak my life in small and significant ways to stay and *feel* relevant—from hanging fresh wallpaper to changing my personal "look," to embarking on new projects, traveling to new places, and expanding my friendships. (Those are just a few examples.) Just as the company has evolved over the past thirty years, so have I.

I'm not afraid to retire an old pattern and make a change, and yet sometimes

> WHEN WE AREN'T OPEN TO CHANGING OUR VIEWS, TAKING CHANCES, AND MOVING FORWARD, WE RUN THE RISK OF BECOMING DISINTERESTED, UNINSPIRED, OR FEELING STUCK IN OUR LIVES.

even I need a reminder or a nudge. I won't forget the time Mother and I showed up to meet each other at a restaurant in Boca Raton and we were both wearing the same Vera Bradley quilted jacket, camisole, and matching skirt—in the same color! She was seventy-five and I was forty-five and we were dressed like twin sisters. We looked at each other and started to laugh. I said, "Mother, I think it's time we get a new look."

WHO DO YOU WANT TO BE TODAY?

To this day, buyers and our own sales department will say, "Give us another Java Blue." They don't actually want another pattern with brown and turquoise because that color combination is no longer on-trend (although that could always change in a season or two). What they mean is: *give us something new and unexpected.*

In what ways can you push the design of your life beyond the familiar and expected? To my mind, personal redesign needn't be huge. It can be subtle, and still significant. What big or small twist on an old pattern can you make that will help you feel more relevant and true to the woman you want to be *today*?

CUT AND TRIM

While I'm often described as impulsive, I do believe that our lives are better by design. That is, when we sketch out how we want our lives to look, and then make a plan to implement that vision, we can accomplish our goals. At Vera Bradley, this is precisely how we design our collections:

Have an idea.

Make a sketch.

Create a plan.

Put the right people in place to help create it.

Stay true to the vision through to the end.

Whatever it is I'm doing, I strive for it to look and feel right. Again, I credit my Catholic upbringing for this. In my high school home-economics class, the nuns who taught us were very particular about the details, especially with sewing projects. They would turn a dress inside out and inspect the construction, finishing, and seams. Sixty percent of our grade was based on what the inside of the piece looked like. If it was sloppy or poorly designed, we were asked to start over.

The nuns taught me that "fine" is never good enough. Over the years, I've created my own adult version that mirrors this attitude: *"fine" is a four-letter word*. Meaning, whatever it is you're designing or building, make it the best that it can be inside and out, through and through. If the outcome is only "fine," then in order to create the dress, handbag, or the *life* that feels and looks just right, you may have to cut and trim. You may just have to take the approach the nuns did, and scrap your original design and start from scratch.

At Vera Bradley, we've recolored prints at the last minute and canceled entire collections that we didn't feel confident about. I've redone booths at the gift shows, reset displays in our showrooms, and pulled products at the eleventh hour to maintain the integrity and the quality of the brand, to stay true to the company's vision and do what's right for the customer. We tweak it until it's right. This can often mean extra work, but we believe it's well worth the time and effort because "fine" is not what we're striving for. Excellence is our goal.

OUR LIVES ARE BETTER BY DESIGN. WHEN WE SKETCH OUT HOW WE WANT OUR LIVES TO LOOK, AND THEN MAKE A PLAN TO IMPLEMENT THAT VISION, WE CAN ACCOMPLISH OUR GOALS.

That said, scrapping your design entirely isn't always necessary. If a plan isn't coming together quite as you'd imagined, there may be an acceptable alternative. If you've moved to a new city and things haven't turned out like you planned, ask yourself if it's the city or maybe just the neighborhood that needs to be reconsidered. If you work for a great company but find yourself looking for more challenges in your day, find a way to take on new responsibilities that may lead to greater opportunities. Try not to confuse a setback with defeat. Instead, consider how you may redesign and work with what you already have. We once ordered the wrong zippers for a bag we were designing. Since it was our mistake, we didn't expect the manufacturer to exchange them. So there we were, stuck with hundreds of sixteen-inch zippers that were too long for our twelve-inch bag. There was only one thing to do: redesign the bag to fit the zipper. We made it work and the "Miller" bag continues to be one of our bestsellers.

At other times, we've had to simply go back to the drawing board and make a few tweaks. I was once in London for Fashion Week with our then head of marketing Sue Britton. She and I had just walked out of an upscale restaurant when I heard a jangling noise coming from the direction of her bag. Sue heard it, too, and we looked at each other in amused disbelief when we realized she had a fork, a knife, and a spoon stuck to the bottom of her Vera Bradley bag. Her table setting from the restaurant! She was carrying a prototype for a new tote we'd designed and the magnet for the fastener-clasp was apparently so strong that it had attracted her silverware.

"We need to get this right before it goes into production." Sue laughed.

"And this ought to teach us to carry samples before they're finished," I said as we turned back toward the restaurant to return the mistakenly stolen goods.

MAKE YOUR LIFE BETTER BY DESIGN

How you design your life is important. Ask yourself, what do I need to cut and trim in my life so that it feels right, or even better? Is there an aspect of your life that doesn't match your original vision or design? Consider the details that will make your life more functional, enjoyable, beautiful, and successful and then sketch it out. Make a plan and rally around you the right people to help you fulfill your vision.

CONTINUE TO REDESIGN

At the end of my life I want to be able to say that I have no regrets. I did what I wanted to do, and I was true to myself—my strengths, passions, needs, and desires. I've redesigned my life many times in an attempt to stay true to me and also to discontinue old patterns that no longer worked.

When Vera Bradley was young, I left my first marriage of twenty-eight years. My husband had sold his company and retired from a long career. He was happy to finally slow down. I, on the other hand, was revving up. I was excited with the new direction my life, and the company, was taking me and I realized I wasn't going to be happy settling for my husband's version of happiness. I wanted something different. I wanted something more.

Still, leaving my marriage was a very difficult decision. In fact, it was the hardest time in my

> I BELIEVE WE SHOULD ALL GIVE OURSELVES PERMISSION TO CHOOSE MORE HAPPINESS.

life. I struggled with many feelings, including doubt and a fear of remorse. Was I being too selfish? Was I breaking up the family? Maybe I should just *stay*. My grown children were furious. They felt blindsided. They protested that we were a solid family and they didn't understand why I wanted to leave. It's true that our marriage did look pretty idyllic from the outside. And though my children were right that we were a good family, we were no longer a great couple. We'd come to a point in our lives where we wanted very different things.

I understood my children's conflict. They were torn between their loyalty to their father and to me, and were also wrestling with the loss of an earlier time when we were all happily together. Ultimately, however, I chose something more for myself. I made a change that I believed would make me happier. To me, this was a change worth making. I believe we should all give ourselves permission to choose more happiness.

And even though it ended, I don't regard my first marriage as a failure. Absolutely not. I don't look back on anything in my life and wish it hadn't happened. If I do that, I'll start undoing some very wonderful things. But I am a firm believer that, for many of us, there come times in our lives when refining, redesigning, and big change is possible, if not essential. Whenever I think back on my difficult decision, I have no regrets. I did what was right for me.

CHOOSE MORE

Being true to the next version of yourself doesn't have to mean leaving a life partner behind. Many of us find our new selves in different locations, jobs, with children, and happily alongside the spouses we chose decades before. But know that whatever version of redesign is meant for you, it's probably not optional when a part of you either whispers or screams out for change. Chances are good that the price of ignoring those promptings may be too costly for you. So listen hard. How is your redesign calling you?

EMBRACE YOUR SUCCESS

Throughout my life, I think about what my mother used to say about embodying confidence any day of the week. "Walk like you smell something burning—quickly and with your head up and your spine straight."

That's how I've tried to carry myself over the course of the growth of Vera Bradley. There have been many moments when I didn't know what was coming. And success didn't happen overnight. Like everything else, it progressed in starts and stops, and grew over time. If, thirty years ago, someone could have given me a sneak peek into the future of where Vera Bradley was headed I would have been terrified. The idea that with our combined five hundred dollars in cash Pat and I would one day have a company generating a half-billion dollars annually would have felt too big. An overwhelming undertaking. I probably would have said, *There's no way we can run a company of that size.* But the company grew at the rate a child does. Gradually. It started out as a seven-pound baby and grew bigger, incrementally, until one day it was six foot two.

I remember the first Vera Bradley quilted handbags in ivory floral blue and rose followed by our first significant order from Nobson's women's store in Fort Wayne. Three decades later, we have one hundred and ten company-owned Vera Bradley stores, forty separate Vera Bradley outlet stores, and twenty-seven hundred independent retail accounts, in addition to top placement at many large department stores. I never imagined we'd be in so many places.

I remember when only our friends and family were carrying our bags. Now three million American women carry Vera Bradley and we're sold in all fifty states, plus Japan, Guam and Canada.

I remember when we were operating out of the windowless upstairs room of my first husband's paper company and now we have a distribution center that ships two million dollars' worth of product a day. I am always amazed when I walk into this over 400,000-square-foot facility and recognize the size of our operation day-to-day. (It blows Costco away!)

You don't necessarily see the growth when you live with something every day. Spend each day with someone, doing something, be it a child, a partner, a creative project, or a business, and growth is a slow and natural progression. In that way, it's much easier to handle and hold. And as it grows, you grow, too. Your arms become stronger, you become smarter, more patient, more insightful, and hopefully more adaptable and competent. Until one day, you look down at your baby, now grown, and realize you carried her all the way. That's when it occurs to you that you were strong all along.

GROWTH IS A SLOW AND NATURAL PROGRESSION. BE PATIENT AND PERSISTENT.

So embrace the success you've earned up until now and pump up your resolve for what comes next. Set aside your fears of "too big" and "too much," and replace them with the idea that you can grow into who you need and want to be. And, above all, embody confidence.

The second part to embracing success is celebrating your success. Once the company actually started making money and I was afforded a weekly, take-home paycheck, I decided to splurge on a beautiful blue, porcelain table lamp. I called Mother after I'd purchased it and she asked, "Where are you going to put it?"

"Probably in the living room."

"No," she said sweetly. "This is for *you*. Put it on your bedroom nightstand. That way it will be the last thing you see before you go to sleep and the first thing you see when you wake up in the morning." I still have that beautiful, colorful lamp and I think about Mother's words—"this is for you"— every time I turn it on.

People often ask me, if Vera were still alive what would she think about how the company has grown, how successful it's become? That's easy—she would embrace it, and she would be proud of how the Vera Bradley sisterhood and products have expanded all over the globe. And positively, she would have happily joined in all the fun.

Every success that the company enjoys, I enjoy for Mother. And the truth is I owe so much of it to her. Vera Bradley was built on her values—kindness, generosity, respect, attention to detail, and a deep belief that there is always a beautiful solution waiting to be found. Many of us have been raised by women who have made us the successful women we are today. If you haven't lately, thank *your* mother. Give credit to those who have made you, *you*.

EMBRACE YOUR SUCCESS AND EMBODY CONFIDENCE.

CELEBRATE EACH AND EVERY SUCCESS

When we've reached our goal, achieved what we've set out to do, or simply had a big breakthrough, it's important to recognize and mark it. Instead of overlooking, dismissing, or plodding forward toward the next thing, take a moment and acknowledge what you've done so far. Embrace and celebrate each and every success. If you don't, who will?

FIND THE SILVER LINING

Most days, I live my life as if things will work out and, for the most part, they do. My life has been blessed in many ways. Still, I've had my share of heartbreak and loss: the death of my dear friend Mary Sloane, Mother's terribly sudden car accident and passing, Peer's devastating diagnosis of Alzheimer's disease.

I saw my first hint of Peer's illness in the early 2000s during a trip to Atlanta for the annual gift show. We'd made plans to meet at the Ritz-Carlton Hotel and Peer went to the wrong one. At the time, I dismissed it and kidded with him. "Why would you go to the one across town when we've been coming to this one for years?" Where his mistake may have seemed like a minor thing to most people, it did catch my attention. It was out of character for him. Here was a man who spoke six languages, ran a successful business, and never missed a beat. *Why would he have gone to the wrong hotel?* After the incident in Atlanta I started paying closer attention to Peer's actions and, more and more, I noticed little slipups. A mispronounced name here. A forgotten detail there. Where his

> I LIVE MY LIFE AS IF THINGS
> WILL WORK OUT, AND FOR
> THE MOST PART, THEY DO.
> MY LIFE HAS BEEN BLESSED
> IN MANY WAYS. STILL,
> I'VE HAD MY SHARE OF
> HEARTBREAK AND LOSS.

recall had always been so sharp, it was starting to soften. Because I knew him so well, I recognized small and subtle changes, like stalling ever-so-slightly before addressing people.

One day while visiting the IU School of Medicine for a meeting of the breast cancer center fund-raising board, I mentioned my worries about Peer to a friend on the board. "He just seems a little off," I said. "He's acting forgetful."

"Bring him in," she encouraged, and a week later Peer agreed to an appointment with a nationally respected neurologist. Where I'd had my suspicions, there was also a part of me that was in denial, that didn't want to accept that anything could be wrong with my husband. So when the diagnosis came back for early Alzheimer's I was devastated. I remember the moment very well. I completely fell apart. I sobbed and apologized at the same time. "This is so unlike me," I cried. "I'm not usually like this." I dropped my head into my hands. "I'm a positive person."

I thought back to when Mother died and I'd had the poise to do her makeup the day of her funeral. But this was hitting me much harder. *Not Peer,* is what I thought. He went through so much. That Peer had defied death in a POW camp during World War II and then to have to suffer from this merciless disease felt so unfair to me. I didn't know anyone who'd had Alzheimer's and once I began to learn more about it, I realized it was the long good-bye. There was no cure and nothing I could do to stop it.

Looking back, I believe that because we had kept separate residences up until this point—Peer in Chicago and me in Fort Wayne—I'd missed out on noticing the warning signs sooner. I didn't see him every day and when we spoke over the phone, he was composed. When we did see each other on the weekends, he appeared in perfect physical health.

Not long after his diagnosis, Peer moved from Chicago to Fort Wayne permanently. It was an uncertain and unsettling time, but Peer kept his sense of humor. "Let's make a deal," he said. "You remember your name and I'll remember mine." Not only funny, he was gracious—always inviting his nurses and doctors to lunch—and also courageous. I recall the day he handed me his car keys. "I shouldn't be driving. I don't want to be responsible for hurting anyone." I was touched that he would take a backseat out of respect for others on the road. Soon after, Gregory moved from Queens to Fort Wayne to help drive Peer to his appointments during the day.

I continued to work full-time at Vera Bradley and Cecylia, my longtime housekeeper who had become a close friend and like a family member herself, cared for Peer when I was at the office. Cecylia, who was not a trained caregiver, tended to him as well as any professional. I wasn't surprised this came naturally to her. I'd observed her deliver the same level of kindness, patience, and care to her Down's syndrome son.

While I was at work, Cecylia kept Peer company—she read to him, took him to lunch, and always treated him with consideration and respect, never like a patient to be pitied. In fact, she was quite sassy with Peer, which he adored. When the illness progressed and robbed more of Peer's independence, Cecylia did for him what he could not do for himself. And still, he was strong to the end.

I have a photograph of Peer and me taken the year he died (page 187). We were down in Seaside, Florida, for a Vera Bradley photo shoot when the photographer snapped a candid picture of the two of us on the beach. You would never know that Peer was sick to look at this image. I'm leaning into him and he's supporting me as

EVEN IN TIMES OF GREAT SADNESS THERE CAN BE BEAUTIFUL MOMENTS.

THE CARE AND KINDNESS OF FRIENDS CAN HELP YOU THROUGH ALMOST ANYTHING.

he always did. Peer exhibited strength of character until the last day of his life.

It's nearly impossible to describe what it's like to watch someone you love so dearly change in front of you. And it's even harder to express the grief that comes after a loss of this kind. The day Peer died, I didn't want to see or talk to any friends or family, which is uncharacteristic of me. But Mac Finley, a friend of my grandson's and who lived in the neighborhood, rode his bicycle over to the house when he heard that Peer had passed away. Cecylia kindly greeted him at the front door and told him that I was resting and not feeling up to visitors. "I won't leave until I can give Birdie a hug," the fourteen-year-old said firmly. When Mac wouldn't leave his position on the front porch, Cecylia told him to wait and then gently knocked on my bedroom door. "Christopher's friend from down the street is here to see you. He says he won't leave until he can give you a hug." *How much he must love Peer and me to make such a stand,* I thought. I left my bedroom for the first time that day and met Mac Finley on the porch. He hugged me tightly and I hugged him back. *Even in grief,* I thought, *there can be beautiful moments.*

What got me through this heartbreaking time was the kindness and care of close family and friends, and my determination and perseverance to find, or rather create, a silver lining in this tragic personal event. I became inspired to create a beautiful day-away center for people with Alzheimer's and dementia. I envisioned a colorful space that felt warm and cozy and that allowed individuals to spend their days comfortably and safely while their loved ones were at work or taking a much needed break.

I deeply understood this need.

Where I had been so fortunate to have the loving and constant presence of Cecylia and others like my brother Eddie and Gregory to help care for Peer, I appreciated that not everyone has this. There had been many times when I walked through the door at the end of the day and thought: *what would I do without their help? Where else would I take him? Where would I feel comfortable leaving him for the day?*

I designed Birchwood exactly as I would have wanted it to look and feel for Peer and me. In fact, it looks a lot like my own home—colorful wallpaper, warm lighting and comfy chairs, throw pillows and blankets in every room.

I took the same "ready, fire, aim" approach to this project as I do to most everything else. If I recognize a need and am passionate about something, I don't wait for a committee to talk me out of it. I take action. Within a year it was up and running. I brought all the right people together—architects, builders, investors, and caregivers—to help create a beautiful and safe retreat for other people like Peer. I won't forget when, soon after it opened, a gentleman whose wife was an Alzheimer's patient said to me, "This is the first time I've left my wife for a day and felt good about it. Thank you." My beloved Peer was gone, but by creating Birchwood, I felt like all was not lost. I'd taken a sad moment and created something hopeful.

FIND THE LIGHT IN THE SHADOWS

I am committed to life. On the grayest of days, I look for the silver lining. Or I add color. How can you turn a challenging personal event into something beautiful, or an avenue to be helpful or of service to others? When you look for the light in the shadows, you often find it.

LEAN ON YOUR SISTERS

Peer died knowing my name and who I was to him. His doctor Marty Farlow said to me, "Most Alzheimer's patients don't have that. You're both lucky and you gave him a great gift—you let him die first." I passed on these words to my dear friend Glenna shortly after Peer passed. "He's right," I agreed as I imagined Peer all alone. "What would he have done if I'd gone before him?"

Glenna lowered her gaze and looked at me over her glasses. "Honey, he'd have been remarried in six months."

You need friends like this in your life, friends who can make you laugh in even the darkest and most challenging times. Glenna always knows the perfect thing to say, and often will say what no one else would dare. I love her for this.

Glenna, whom the "Glenna" bag is named after, and I have been friends since Marymount College. We arrived as freshmen and met at the first school assembly. Glenna tells the story of walking into a packed auditorium and spotting me across the room. A natural blonde from Grosse Pointe, Michigan, Glenna

YOU NEED FRIENDS WHO CAN MAKE YOU LAUGH IN EVEN THE DARKEST AND MOST CHALLENGING TIMES.

thought to herself, *how in the heck is that redhead more tanned than me?* Because I was from Miami Beach and used to rub baby oil all over my body to get tan would have been my answer.

Glenna and I gravitated toward each other, I think, because we share a similar sense of humor and a positive attitude. Glenna truly looks on the bright side, and has a sunny disposition whatever the weather.

Glenna and I lived together in the dorms with Mary Sloane through our second year at Marymount, before I switched to Barat College in Lake Forest, Illinois. Despite the distance, we all remained close friends. I continued to invite them both down to my parents' Miami Beach home during spring break where we'd frequent the bars in Fort Lauderdale at night and fry our skin on the beaches during the day. (This concerned Vera, the former Elizabeth Arden model, very much, by the way.)

My friends Glenna, Mary, and Mary Ann were some of the first Vera Bradley sales reps. They helped Pat and me work many of the early gift shows, and it was often Glenna who encouraged us at four-thirty in the afternoon to start serving cocktails to the vendors next door, as well as to the buyers walking by. Glenna and I have remained steady in each other's lives for nearly five decades now, and our husbands—Peer and John—also became good friends along the way. Some of my fondest memories are of the four of us ringing in the New Year at the Drake Hotel in Chicago.

Like me, Glenna surrounds herself with color and doesn't get stuck for too long in the dark. "You don't come out of hard times," she says, "you push through them." When our friend Mary died from breast cancer, Glenna and I held each other up. Years later, when Glenna was similarly diagnosed with cancer, we fought against it with our combined lightness and laughter. To this day, we crack up about the time I drove to Ann Arbor to sit with Glenna during one of her routine chemo treatments. We were in a communal room with other cancer patients receiving IV drips when we got to kidding around and laughing so hard we were crying. The next time I visited her during treatment, the attending nurse put Glenna in a small private room.

"Thank you, dear," Glenna said. "But I don't need a separate room."

The nurse's reply: "Oh, yes, you do. Not everyone laughs through chemo as much as the two of you."

Laughter is magic medicine, and sometimes, laughing is all you can really do. At Peer's funeral, Glenna helped me to be lively and light, so much so that at one point I asked the funeral director if he thought we were acting insensitive. "Absolutely not," he responded. "I judge how much someone was loved by how much laughter there is in the room. It's an indicator of how much happiness this person brought into all of your lives, and the amount of connectedness you shared."

When Glenna's darling husband, John Reno, passed away from cancer and she was grieving, I went to her bedside, pulled back the covers, and crawled in next to her. Over the years, Glenna had joked that if something should ever happen to her, I should marry her husband, John, but now here we were—both of us widows. I held her tightly and whispered in her ear, "Now what's wrong with this picture? I'm supposed to be in bed with John, not you."

I hope for every woman to have a friendship like Glenna and I have. In my life, my friends have been there for me through every milestone moment, and I often call on different friends for different reasons. Where Glenna is my go-to for levity and humor, Mary Ann is one of my oldest confidants, and Cecylia is my truth-teller. You need that friend who can tell you to put lipstick on, or that your favorite jeans are no longer working for you, just as you need the friend

> LAUGHTER IS MAGIC MEDICINE, AND SOMETIMES, LAUGHING IS ALL YOU CAN REALLY DO.

from whom you have no secrets, and where you can be your most vulnerable self. Mary Ann is that friend for me. We've spent forty-one summers as next-door neighbors on Lake Gage. Our children and grandchildren have grown up together and we've spent countless hours on the dock talking about every aspect of our lives, including our shared style in fashion and decorating. There is nothing about me she doesn't know, and she'd probably say the same about me. In addition to friends like Mary Ann, with whom I share a long history, I also think it's important to have friends that are just easy to *be* with. I have friends I like to shop with, others I prefer to take walks with, and some I love to the moon and back, but don't want to go on vacation with. In my opinion, there's no one-size-fits-all friendship, just as there's no one style of handbag that suits every woman. *If only! Our Vera Bradley collection would be much simpler to create.* But the reality is: we each need a sisterhood to help us carry our bags.

Whenever I'm approached for relationship advice (remember: I have an open-door policy and all topics are welcome), I caution against leaning on our spouses or partners to be our "best friend." It's unfair and unreasonable, isn't it, to expect our romantic partners to be everything to us? How can they be? They're only one person. Why set them up to fail?

Where Peer was my perfect companion, I've always needed my girlfriends to keep me company, too. And maybe that's because I am, at heart, a girl's girl. As I do with many things, I credit this to my upbringing. I grew up with three sisters and spent summers throughout my adolescence and young adulthood at an all-girls camp where "girls rule."

My sister Joan and I started attending Camp We-Ha-Kee in Marinette, Wisconsin, together when I was eight years old and she was ten. Getting there involved a two-day train ride from Miami to Chicago, and then another six hours to the Wisconsin-Michigan border. Camp We-Ha-Kee was a magical place, and quite a departure from my life on the beach. For starters, it was run by some

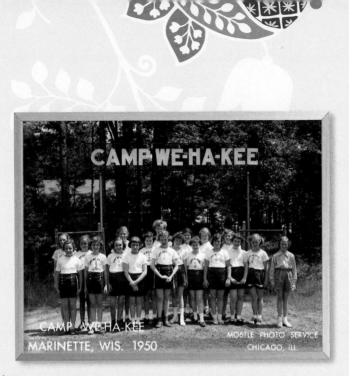

My experiences at summer camp taught me

how to create a sisterhood.

Having fun with two of my sisters, 1955.

WE EACH NEED A SISTERHOOD TO HELP US CARRY OUR BAGS.

of the most fun-loving Dominican nuns you'll ever meet who taught us sportsmanship, leadership, fierce independence and, above all, how to create and foster a sisterhood.

In the early years, Vera and Ed would drop us off and then we often wouldn't see them again until two months later when they picked us up. Now, this was before e-mail and texting so once we were at camp, we were more or less on our own. I remember when I first told my own children about our long summers at camp and they looked at me in horror. Two whole months without Mom and Dad! To them, this sounded like child neglect. But I never saw it that way. I held no resentment toward my parents for "sending us to camp." Quite the opposite. My sisters and I couldn't wait to get there and often cried when Mother and Dad showed up at the end of summer to bring us home.

Eventually all four Bradley girls would attend Camp We-Ha-Kee. I went for ten years and then I became a camp counselor. The last summer I spent at camp was my freshman year of college. It's no surprise, when I think back to these many years at camp, that I would eventually form a company built on solid friendships, teamwork, and *fun,* and where our annual outlet sale attracting "sisters" from all across the map feels very much like a camp revival.

When my female colleagues and I sit around the office talking about the delicate balance of our lives, I'm sometimes asked how I find the time to maintain my close friendships.

"I *make* the time to reach out," I say. "A quick phone call, a goofy text, Bitmoji, or by the old-fashioned way—putting a card or handwritten note in the mail."

After all, this is how my camp sisters and I learned to stay in touch.

GIRLS (REALLY DO) RULE

Make time to cultivate your female friendships in their many and varied forms. Reach out to them, even in a small way: a text, a phone call, a note. (I have a stash of cards in my office drawer to pull from. My favorite reads: *I thought of you a hundred times today.*) Lean on your sisters. And let them know that they can lean on you.

NOTICE THE MAGICAL MOMENTS

During the month of May, many of the residents of Fort Wayne, Indiana, proudly show their support in the fight against breast cancer with beautiful pink-ribbon pathways set up throughout our hometown. This monthlong event, called Turn the Town Pink, was created by the Vera Bradley Foundation for Breast Cancer, and every pink ribbon donated is dedicated to someone who battled the disease.

Several years ago I was driving to the office on a particularly misty spring morning. I turned onto a long stretch of road that borders the Sycamore Hills Golf Club, where hundreds of pink ribbons were staked every two feet up and down the course. As I drove along, one ribbon that had fallen off its stake caught my eye. It was laying all by itself on the ground, so I pulled my car over and jogged across the street to pick it up. As I secured it back in place I couldn't help but notice the name on the ribbon: MARY SLOANE.

What were the odds?

WE ARE ALL CONNECTED BY INVISIBLE THREADS.

There were hundreds of ribbons on this stretch of road, and hers was the one that had fallen? I felt strongly that Mary was right there with me, as if to say, *Thank you. Keep doing what you're doing, Barbie.*

There have been too many coincidences like this one in my life for me to believe they're simply funny luck. In fact, so many situations, people, and events have lined up in my life at just the right time and in just the right way that I'm convinced my life has been blessed with some kind of magic. When he was younger, my grandson Henry referred to these moments as "g' dinky winks," his version of a more familiar phrase—God winks.

While I rely on spirituality more than on any one religious path, I do believe that the divine does often intervene by positioning people and creating situations in our lives when we need them most, connecting us by those invisible threads I've talked about. In my experience, the more you expect life to magically—and colorfully—come together, the more it does. Remember: positivity is one of my strengths, and the days when things don't go well, I say: *God, you've got the wrong person!*

Vera always told me I was lucky. I used to wonder if that was why she'd ask me to pick her lottery numbers. But I believe it went deeper than luck; I think Mother recognized in me something she expressed as well—a willingness to see the magical moments in every day.

EXPECT MAGIC

Look around. Take notice of the people, situations, and opportunities in your life that seem to magically appear, or come to your attention at just the right time—when you need them and desire them most. Your next redesign starts with seizing, and acting upon, those moments. I believe we are each capable of creating the life we want. We can each be more, create more and do more. Take a deep breath and start before you stop, now.

ACKNOWLEDGMENTS

I believe in giving credit where it's due, and this book would not have been possible without the collaborative strengths and contributions of so many talented people. For starters, a big thank-you to my son-in-law and president of the Vera Bradley board, Bob Hall, who without his encouragement (and relentless pestering), I would not have written this book. Bob made all the right connections to make *A Colorful Way of Living* what it has become. I'm grateful for his introduction to my top-notch literary agent, Yfat Reiss Gendell at Foundry Literary + Media, who had a vision for this project from day one and who has welcomed me into the exciting world of publishing. Thanks also to editorial associate Jessica Felleman; the foreign rights team of Kirsten Neuhaus and Heidi Gall; the contracts team of Deirdre Smerillo, Melissa Moorehead, and Hayley Burdett; and the finance team of Sara DeNobrega and Alex Rice.

Next to Samantha Rose, my cowriter, who made this collaboration another fun and unforgettable story in my life—thank you! You have my deepest gratitude and appreciation. You supported and encouraged me throughout these many months and were able to express my thoughts and memories beautifully. As the book came to life, so did our friendship. I'm forever grateful.

My gratitude for editorial expertise extends to Brenda Copeland, Executive Editor at St. Martin's Press, for her positive attitude, unwavering enthusiasm, and clear eye for detail (a woman after my own heart!). Thank you so much for your attention to and love for my stories, and also to your assistant, Maggie Callan, and the entire St. Martin's team who have given so much of their time and energy to making this book look and read just right—copy editor NaNá V. Stoelzle; production editor Lauren Hougen; director of publicity Tracey Guest; publicist Jessica Lawrence; director of marketing and associate publisher Laura Clark; marketing manager Karlyn Hixon; publisher Sally Richardson; publisher's assistant Chris Holder; editorial director George Witte; head of sales Alison Lazarus; account reps Brad Wood and Jeanette Zwart; subrights professional Gisela Ramos; director of art department Michael Storrings; Donna Sinisgalli and Danielle Fiorella, designers. You all embrace my belief that "fine" is never good enough. Thank you for your standard of excellence and attention to every colorful detail.

And finally in the editorial department, a special thanks to my dear friend Joan Maxwell who knows me so well. Thank you for your keen insights, and for helping me to remember and refine my best stories.

Next, to my family, who have put their hands and hearts into building Vera Bradley. The company, and the stories throughout these pages, would not be what they are (or exist at all) without you. My appreciation extends beyond words.

To my parents Vera and Ed, who blessed my life. I think of you every day.

To my husband Peer, for being my strongest supporter. I won the lottery with you.

To my children:

Joanie, for your perspective, and for all the fun and adventure we have in Montana, New York, and everywhere in between.

Amy, for getting it done. You are always there when I need you—my friend, my neighbor, my meals on wheels.

Tommy, for your incredible sense of humor, style, and great taste.

Jimmy, for your optimism and for being my glass FULL kid.

To my niece Kathy Ray, you've always been more like a daughter to me.

To my son-in-law, Mike Ray, for your strength and leadership, and for following your dream of running a women's handbag company (wink) and taking Vera Bradley to the next level.

To my daughters-in-law, Laura and Marlo, for keeping my sons in line. Thank you.

To my grandchildren: Christopher, Frannie, Stepper, Molly, Eddie, Teddy, Henry, Maggie, John, Bradley, Gavin, and Audrey. I am so grateful for all the wonderful memories (and many more to come!). And to all my honorary grandchildren (you know who you are)—you ALL fill my heart with joy every time I hear you call me Birdie.

And to my sisters Joan, Susan, and Kathy, and my brothers Ed and Jamie, who share in all the incredible memories of my childhood. Weren't we lucky!

To my partner, Pat Miller, who knocked on my door those many years ago and shared in all the fun and joy of creating Vera Bradley. Thanks for the memories.

To Debbie Wilson—what would I do without you?

To Kim Colby—thank you for keeping the f in fun every day for over thirty years. You are one of the biggest reasons I love coming to work every day.

To Veronique—you keep the f in French. Next to Peer, you're my favorite European.

And to my working family—past and present—who have made Vera Bradley a sisterhood, and a company to be proud of, and to the Vera Bradley Board of Directors who have been totally supportive every step of the way, and haven't fired me yet.

Next, to my dear friends Mary Sloane, Glenna Reno, and Mary Ann Gray, and my sister Joan Reedy, who jumped on board when Vera Bradley was just an idea and believed in me to follow my dream, and to all my friends who make my life colorful every day. To Anne Frantz, for bringing our stores to life. I cherish our friendship. To David Goodman (you'll always be Albert to me) and Cyrus Cooley—thanks for the endless laughs. You keep me young!

To Marymount College for bringing lasting friendships to my life, and to Camp We-Ha-Kee for teaching me the true meaning of team spirit.

To Sherry and Mike Holifield, thank you for maintaining the dignity of Baekgaard Limited and keeping Peer's dream alive. To Cecylia DeLucca and Dawn Nolan—you were there when we needed you the most. I'm eternally grateful.

To the Vera Bradley Breast Cancer Foundation, I thank the many employees, volunteers, and anyone who has ever bought a pink ribbon symbolizing your genuine commitment, energy, and passion toward our mission to save lives and project a vision of hope.

To the amazing medical professionals at Indiana University who have always been there for us. To Mary Maxwell and Liz Elkas, for always answering our calls, and to Dr. Marty Farlowe and Elva Van Hook, for your compassion and friendship toward Peer and me.

A special thanks to Jill Nichols who brought to my attention the need for the day-away facility that became Birchwood, and to everyone who gave tirelessly and put their heart into this personal project of mine.

Thank you, Fort Wayne, for supporting us every step of the way.

Thank you, New York City, for your energy and inspiration.

And, last but not least, thank you to the genius who invented the dimmer switch. I sing your praises every day.

AUTHOR BIO

Barbara Bradley Baekgaard

Cofounder, Chief Creative Officer, and Director

Ms. Baekgaard cofounded Vera Bradley in 1982. From 1982 through June 2010, she served as copresident. In May 2010, she was appointed chief creative officer. She currently serves as a board member of the Indiana University Melvin and Bren Simon Cancer Center Development Board and the Vera Bradley Foundation for Breast Cancer.

Ms. Baekgaard has earned industry recognition and received numerous awards, including the Entrepreneur of the Year Award for the State of Indiana from Arthur Young/VENTURE in 1987 (awarded jointly with Ms. Miller), the Gifts and Decorative Accessories Industry Achievement Award in 2006, the Country Living Entrepreneur Award in 2007, and the Lifetime Achievement Award from AmericasMart/Icon Honors in 2014. In August 2016, Ms. Baekgaard accepted the ACE Humanitarian Award from the Accessories Council in New York City.

When she has time to take a break from her busy schedule, Ms. Baekgaard enjoys traveling and spending time with her friends, her four children, and her twelve grandchildren.

Pat Miller, cofounder, retired in 2012 and remains a member of the Vera Bradley board of directors.

COMPANY BIO

Vera Bradley is a leading designer, producer, marketer, and retailer of a wide offering of handbags, accessories, and travel and leisure items that complement many of the milestone moments of our lives. Over its thirty-three-year history, Vera Bradley has become a true lifestyle brand with a loyal following of women of all ages.